7 STEPS TO EFFECTIVE COMMUNICATION

7 STEPS TO EFFECTIVE COMMUNICATION

JAMES WILLIAM SELLS

FORUM HOUSE/PUBLISHERS
Atlanta

Copyright © FORUM HOUSE 1973

All rights reserved.

No part of this book may be reproduced in any form, except for brief quotations in reviews, without the written permission of Forum House, Inc., Atlanta.

Library of Congress Catalog Card Number
72-97820
ISBN 0-913618-04-7
ISBN 0-913618-17-9 paperback

ACKNOWLEDGMENTS

From *Talk That Gets Results* by K. C. Ingram. Copyright 1957, McGraw-Hill Book Company.

From *Aurora Leigh* by Elizabeth Barrett Browning. Copyright 1966 Oxford Dictionary of Quotations. Used with permission of Oxford University Press.

For my wife, Vera,
    our daughter, Jeanne (1932-1955),
    and her son, James Robert Adams,
Jr.

Contents

FOREWORD	ix
INTRODUCTION	xiii
STEP ONE: PREPARE	1
PRACTICE EXERCISES	19
STEP TWO: LISTEN	22
PRACTICE EXERCISES	37
STEP THREE: "READ"	41
PRACTICE EXERCISES	55
STEP FOUR: GAIN ATTENTION	58
PRACTICE EXERCISES	70
STEP FIVE: DECLARE	72
PRACTICE EXERCISES	84
STEP SIX: INTERPRET	88
PRACTICE EXERCISES	104
STEP SEVEN: ASK FOR ACTION	107
PRACTICE EXERCISES	120
ADDENDUM 1: SEVEN STEPS AND THE JOURNEY	122
ADDENDUM 2: TEN COMMANDMENTS OF CHRISTIAN COMMUNICATION	127

FOREWORD

Many books have been written about the principles of communication. Communication is vital—without it, people would be entombed within themselves.

Many books have also been written about Christian principles, another vital subject, and without this guidance, millions of lives would be poorer. The genius of Dr. Sells' book is that it combines the principles of communication with Christian principles. It excites us to anticipate the enrichment that lies ahead for those who will read the book and put its principles into practice in their everyday lives.

BEN C. JOHNSON
Director, Institute
of Church Renewal

IN APPRECIATION

"No man is an island. . ." How true this is in person-to-person communication. This book recaptures the experiences of many friends and acquaintances, as well as my own, and my thanks to each of you, wherever you are. I also express grateful appreciation to the officers and editors of Forum House for their encouragement and assistance.

JAMES WILLIAM SELLS

Introduction

We've all admired persons who communicate smoothly and effectively. Often, such persons have a flair for verbal exchange (a gift of gab), but when you look into their backgrounds, you find either formal training or disciplined self-education. The successful communicators have acquired an understanding of the principles of communication and have practiced the skills. (In communication, as in any other enterprise, a mediocre input produces a mediocre product.)

You, too, can be a smooth and effective communicator — not merely in terms of making a better speech when the occasion arises, but also (and especially) in your daily pursuits. This book will lead you, step by step, to an understanding of how it's done. At the conclusion of each step (or chapter), you'll find suggestions for putting into practice what you've learned.

The word "communication" embraces a broad and diverse field of pursuits, including highly technical media and disciplines — for example, radio, television, advertising, and publishing. These segments of the communication field are beyond the intent and scope of this book. Here we're going to focus on communication between persons in daily situations — we're aiming to help *you* regardless of your age, occupation, sex, marital status, or whichever side of the tracks you live on. Whatever your "thing," you'll enjoy doing it more once you've mastered the art and craft of communication.

You'll be happy to find that the book isn't ponderous — rather, it's a simple guide for the enrichment of human relationships. All you need to master the subject is the book, a few fellow human beings of your choosing, and the interest. You set the pace. Some persons who already have considerable knowledge and skill may choose to complete the seven steps in seven hours. But you can take seven days — or seven weeks.

The seven steps are: (1) prepare; (2) listen; (3) "read"; (4) gain attention; (5) declare; (6) interpret; (7) ask for action.

Mastering these seven steps will provide rich rewards. You can convey and receive information more efficiently — achieve freer exchanges of ideas — enhance friendships — muster the courage to establish new relationships — transact your business or run your home more effectively — be a better member or leader of your church, club, or other organization — become a better citizen — enrich your spiritual life.

Actually, this book could have had any of a number

of titles — some of them a bit zany. For example:

How To Get Your Idea Across Without Polluting the World with Words

Letting the Boss Know What You Think — Without Getting Fired

Getting the Sleepers Awake and Onto the Edge of Their Chairs

How To Make "No" Sound as Palatable as "Yes"

Don't Wait Until You Hit the Divorce Court To Communicate

If You're a Human Being, Why Not Sound Like One?

Poor communication is a favorite topic with cartoonists, stand-up comics, and those hilarious TV characters. But poor communication is no joke. It can cost you much in terms of time, money, embarrassment, estrangement, and wasted potential.

If you're still wavering in commitment, take these two-minute tests:

During the last few days, have you
- lost the drift of a conversation, thus facing the dilemma of whether to forego what was said or to request a replay?
- had an argument with a member of your family because he or she misunderstood you?
- begun an important assignment only to find that you didn't recall the instructions?
- failed to come on strong enough in group conversation to command attention?
- felt inadequate while planning an oral presentation?
- lost your temper because somebody seemed to be blaming you?

interrupted someone, causing him to lose his train of thought?

If you have answered "yes" to any of these questions, this book is for you.

Now, the second test:
- Are you able to read "body language"?
- Do you know how to interrupt someone without being rude?
- Do your facial expressions say what you want them to say?
- Does your conversational ability win and keep friends?
- Are you able to foresee impending disruptions and either head them off or minimize their effect?
- When a group strays from a problem, or bogs down, can you come to the rescue by summarizing the discussion and outlining the options?
- Can you capture elements of agreement between yourself and an antagonist and use this common ground to advance your objective?

If you've answered "no" to any of these questions, again this book is for you. On the other hand, you *don't* need this book *if* you are confident about your communication situation — and *if* your confidence is well founded. These are big *if's*!

Let me confess that although I've been a professional communicator for half a century, I'm always learning new and better ways to build or improve person-to-person bridges. And I'd venture to say there isn't a single relationship in *your* life, either, that can't be improved through better communication.

A life can be no richer than its relationships. Resolve now to enrich your relationships and your life. Here's to your success!

JAMES WILLIAM SELLS

STEP 1 PREPARE

To prepare is
- . to anticipate
- . to plan
- . to put things (and oneself) in readiness
- . to practice

A high-powered training expert had just completed a grueling three-day workshop on communication in sales. He had spent much of the time trying to strengthen the participants' motivation.

A janitor who had been on hand during all of the lectures and discussions was helping the expert pack his equipment. He complimented the expert on his performance and asked if he might ask a question.

"Sure," the expert replied.

"I don't want to make you mad . . ."

"No, that's all right. Go ahead."

"Well," the janitor said, "why does it take you three days to tell these fellows what they need to know?"

The expert was surprised and annoyed. "Because that's my method, that's why. Doesn't my method make sense?"

"You did a good job, all right," said the janitor. "But I could have done the whole thing in one sentence."

The expert swallowed hard. He picked up a piece of chalk and handed it to the janitor. "Okay, show me!"

The janitor stepped to the chalkboard and wrote: "You got to want to."

This is where we begin. *You got to want to.* You have to want to communicate. You have to want to enter into exchanges with other persons. You have to be willing to expend effort and to risk; at times, you must also be willing to exercise patience and restraint. You have to want to improve, and believe that you *can* improve. You can!

First, let's look at some definitions and underlying principles.

Communication is the process which enables persons to (1) exchange ideas, feelings, and information; (2) resolve differences and enhance understanding; (3) build better relationships.

Communication is sending out, and receiving, waves. There are many modes of communication — many types of waves. Each type has its own purpose.

You use one kind of wave when you wish to communicate with a pet animal. When you speak or gesture, the animal responds in obedience or appreciation — or belligerence.

Step One: Prepare

Then there's the wave you use to "talk" to yourself. In polite circles, this is called "internalizing," but we've all seen a person walking along acting out both sides of a debate. (Discretion in your wave selection makes for acceptance rather than eyebrow-raising.)

There are also the waves employed by the communications industry. These media profit by eliciting a favorable response from you. These waves usually travel in one direction — from the medium to the consumer. (But there was this lady who complained, "I haven't had anybody to talk to all day except the television set.") The television station wants you to remain glued to your set and to its channel. A book publisher wants you to pick up his volume, buy it, read it, tell others about it.

Another mode which has traditionally been a one-way channel comprises lectures, sermons, and the like. Information is imparted, counsel given, or reprimands issued, usually with little or no opportunity for you to talk back.

In this book, we won't spend much time on pets, selling goods on the air, or pursuing the lecture circuit. Instead, we will focus on *person-to-person* communication — a universal concern.

We'll talk mainly about oral and written communication; deliberate body language (planned gestures and touch); less overt body signals (a raised eyebrow); and subtle signals such as grooming and dress. Of course, there has to be internalizing — being receptive, "reading" the environment, and planning a response. We recognize the importance of silent mind-to-mind sharing (the mere presence of a friend can be more comforting than a thousand words), and we will talk about employing silence. However, we cannot deal with ESP (extrasensory perception), as such.

Person-to-person communicating is highly individualized. You have your own preferred methods of transmitting, and your "listener" has his own quirks about receiving. This makes person-to-person communication at once both a challenge and a source of joy. The purpose of person-to-person communication is to develop the capacity for understanding — and understanding is the result of effective communication.

The following analogy points up the individualistic and fragile nature of person-to-person communication:

You live in a castle. This castle is composed of building blocks from your total experience — your heredity, your environment, your spiritual input, and your responses to these influences. Your castle is largely of your own making. You have, consciously and unconsciously, built the walls — experience on experience, idea on idea, dream on dream.

Around your castle is a moat, which you have dredged to protect your inner self. Your moat can be crossed only by way of a drawbridge, which you keep raised until such time as you choose to lower it.

Every other person has his own castle, fashioned after his life-style. His castle has a moat, too. And, like yours, it's equipped with a drawbridge.

For the other person to enter your castle, you have to let down your drawbridge; for you to enter his castle, he has to accommodate you in the same way. As much as you may wish to communicate with this other person, you cannot do so if he is unwilling to partici-

Step One: Prepare

pate. (Dr. Paul Tillich said that "communication is participation.")

You cannot storm the other person's castle; you cannot invade his inner self without his permission. *Mutuality* is a condition of letting down drawbridges. "You come over and visit with me in my castle and I'll visit with you in yours. You reveal something of yourself to me and I'll reveal something of myself to you."

But you can't always merely *presume* that the other person will want to participate, reveal, share, discuss, interpret. For you to be permitted to enter his castle and do these things, you may have to lay a careful strategy. You first have to learn something about the peculiarities of this person and his castle. And while it's almost always worthwhile to solicit entry to the other person's castle, occasionally there will be rebuff, disappointment, embarrassment. Sometimes you will have to fall back and regroup.

Communication is a challenge, but well worth the effort. A single good idea may win entrance into a castle for you — and it might be a castle that will change your life.

Successful communication derives from a strange mix of the scientific with the practical. There are times when you take important communication problems into your "laboratory," where you analyze, draw conclusions, draft a plan, and then put the plan into operation. More often, we employ the trial-and-error method (which also, if done well, has scientific overtones). We note that which works, and we appropriate it for later use. Or, we note that which doesn't work, and we discard it. Also, we "fly by the seat of our pants"; that is, we're forever improvising as we go in order to cope with shifting conditions.

In general, this book will encourage you to be much more scientific in your approach to important matters, and a bit more scientific in your approach to lesser matters. Just learning to take five seconds for reflection before speaking to an issue which is worthy of a deliberate response can prove invaluable. If you will at first strive to be more scientific in many of your communication experiences, then you'll find yourself getting the hang of it, and you'll absorb an orderly orientation into your bones. With experience, you'll become faster on your feet, and much more successful. At the same time, we would not want to detract from the values of intuitive and natural responses when these are appropriate. Life would be too tedious if you were forever running back and forth between where you are and "the laboratory."

Let's try our hand at a communications problem.

Say you've found just the used car you need. It's on Honest John's lot. But you live in a small town, where everyone knows everyone else, and you know that Honest John is a Democrat. More important, he knows that you are a Republican. Honest John isn't an ordinary Democrat, but a *rabid* Democrat. He *hates* Republicans!

If you were paying cash, you might just screw up your courage, walk into Honest John's office, plunk down the money, and either (a) drive off before politics can come into the conversation, or (b) dig in and fight. But, alas! you have a car you want to trade in, and you've got to have a good deal or you can't afford the

Step One: Prepare 7

new car. This makes you more dependent upon Honest John's feelings toward you; it also suggests lengthy negotiations.

Let's look at some terms. First, you have a *goal*. A goal is an intention to bring about a well-defined result within a specified period of time. In this instance, your goal is to obtain the new car on a good trade basis, and you want the new car before the weekend.

You have a goal, and you have it in mind. So far, so good. But your problem is that attempting to achieve your goal threatens other dimensions of your life. You are a Republican, you have the convictions of a Republican, and you're proud of this affiliation. You also have character; you aren't going to lie about your party preference (it wouldn't do any good, anyhow), and you don't relish the thought of even acting as though party affiliation makes very little difference to you.

A goal and the pursuit of that goal, then, have to be compatible with your life-position, *who you are*. At this, the ultimate level of self-knowing and judgment-making, we're talking about *purpose*. You want that car (that's your goal), but you refuse to betray your *purpose* in order to get it at a bargain. (Between purpose and goal, there is an intermediate level called *objectives*, and we'll talk about these later.)

You take this car problem into your "communication lab." You analyze, form hypotheses, come up with possible strategies and tactics. As with many communication problems, this one is complex and complicated. There are many variables and imponderables.

You aren't positive that Honest John will bring up

politics, but your "reading" is that he probably will. Anyhow, you'll have to be prepared for such a contingency.

One possible approach would be to say, "Look, John, I just don't want to talk about politics — besides, I'm in a hurry." No — that certainly won't jolly him up.

Another approach would be to take command of the conversation and hold it. Like yourself, John is an enthusiastic gardener. If you talk about tulips and turnips (rather nonpartisan items), you'll establish a fraternal feeling, get your car, and maybe form a friendship for life. In the future, John will want to know how your tulips, turnips, and *car* are coming along.

A good tactic, but you will still have to have a Plan B, just in case . . .

And so you decide that *if* the subject of politics does come up, you will be honest — not aggressive (you aren't about to convert John, anyway), but forthright. You will compliment John on his interest in political affairs — and, "Yes, the Democrats really did lay it on us Republicans in the last local election." Your strategy will be to try to avoid political talk, and to use gardening as a diversion. But if politics does come up, you will evidence your respect for John's right to choose, and you will assume a posture which suggests your belief that John respects your integrity, too. This atmosphere of mutual regard, if cultivated, may sometime permit a discussion of specific issues.

If all goes well, you will obtain your goal (the car, at a bargain, *now*). If things don't go well, at least you will have preserved your self-respect; you will have remained true to yourself at the ultimate level, the level of pur-

Step One: Prepare

pose, which is more important than any car. Manipulation — shading the truth — these tactics may occasionally win a skirmish, but they lose the war!

The first step in effective communication is to prepare. (You don't just barge into Honest John's office.) And the first phase of preparation is to determine what it is you want and whether you're willing and able to pay the price, whether in terms of money, effort, discipline, compromise, or whatever.

In goal-setting, these guidelines apply:
- Clearly define and delineate the end-result you seek.
- Place the end-result within a time reference.
- Test the goal in terms of your interests and resources.
- Test the goal in terms of your *purpose* and *objectives*.

The *purpose* of a children's hospital may be to bring children and the broader community to a higher level of health. Such a children's hospital may have three *objectives*: To carry on superb programs in each of three areas: patient care, education, and research. (There could be more objectives, or fewer.) Moving on down the line, one of the hospital's *goals* may be: To add two beds to the intensive care ward by the end of the year.

Purpose, then, is a statement of who we are and what we're about. For a corporation, purpose is closely tied to "corporate image." For the Christian, purpose is a reading of what God wants us to be in this, our time.

Objectives are expressions of purpose. Objectives project purpose into the realm of doing — they are the bones and muscles of purpose. Still, they are usually more general and usually they project through a longer period of time.

I may seem to be belaboring purpose, objectives, and goals, but I do so for a reason. And let me hasten to say that I'm not trying to be sticky about definitions. You can call purpose "focus," and you can call objectives and goals "long-range and short-range intentions." The names don't matter, as long as we understand each other. My real concern is that many persons attempt important communication efforts without first knowing (1) who they are, (2) what they want, and (3) how they'll go about bringing their dream into reality. You have to care enough to prepare. And your plans must be logical, manageable, and reasonable.

A good leader will occasionally remind his group of its reason for being — he will imbue the group with a sense of destiny. Beyond this, he will encourage the group to revise or reaffirm its objectives, while remaining true to its sense of purpose. (*Purposes* may change, too, but proposed shifts are approached more deliberately.) And, finally, he facilitates the translation of purpose and objectives into "bite-size" chunks of "doing," whether the doing is self-development or external activity.

An "alive" person carries on essentially the same kind of process within himself and with individual friends.

Preparation is the base for your whole communication structure. And if you plan to build high, the base must be broad and solid. Why do we slight preparation in the area of communication? Perhaps it's because we confuse *talking* with *communication*, and *talking* comes naturally. But look at some preparations that we accept as essential to other areas of our lives:

Step One: Prepare

As you prepare to go to a baseball game, you consider the weather. Should you take along heavier clothing? A slicker or umbrella? What are your plans following the game? Should you leave word that you'll be late getting home?

If you are preparing for a camping-fishing trip, a multitude of things must be planned. Are you camping out or staying in a snug cabin? Dry fly or wet fly fishing? Plugs or spinners? Do you have directions or a map? What food will you take?

How about preparing for a golf game? You may have spent *years* perfecting your form and accumulating your gear!

Each morning you prepare for work. This is an involved process although you do it so often you take it for granted. You groom yourself — if you are a man, you shower and shave; if a woman, you also apply make-up to suit your taste and the position you fill. When you arrive at work, you arrange your desk or get out your tools. You schedule your priorities. How much do you plan to accomplish before lunch? If Mr. Brown is out of town and your meeting is postponed, what is your alternate plan? (You have planned, haven't you?) Whom will you meet at lunch? What are his/her interests? Golf? Cooking?

You prepare to leave work, straightening your area. You prepare to go out in the evening. You return home and prepare for bed.

Imagine the concerns about preparation that run through the mind of a woman as she plans for a date with a new man in her life:

What do I really know about him? Should I consult a

mutual friend and learn more about him?

What will help (or hinder) our conversation tonight?

Do I respect and admire him? How shall I signal these feelings to him? Can I be honest and open and yet maintain my integrity?

Am I concerned about letting him know how important he is to me, or am I really more interested in making him understand how *important I am*?

Every day, we receive signals that say, "Prepare." A buzzer tells us to look into the oven; a bell tells us to come into the classroom. And there are more subtle signals: The dimming of the lights in the symphony hall prepares you for the concert. The overture prepares you for the opera. At the Sunday morning service, the prelude prepares you to worship.

If people were all alike, preparation for communication would be simple, but they are not — they come in infinite varieties. Or, if situations were all alike, again preparation would be much simpler, but there are infinite varieties of settings and conditions. So, you are always making preparations at many levels, especially the *general* level and at the *specific* level.

At the general level, you can prepare by understanding "people." From your knowledge of how you react and your observations of how people about you have reacted in the past, you extrapolate that Mr. Jones can be expected to react thusly to given stimuli in a given setting. A good student of group dynamics can make similar assumptions about groups of people in terms of how they'll interact. General assumptions are helpful, even though any assumption you launch may be shot down by exceptions.

Step One: Prepare 13

From this base of generalities, you make your excursions into the specific. You are not dealing with "people," but with individual "persons," or groups of persons. Who is this person? What are his needs? What are his interests? How does he operate? What is his mind set — open, closed, or tentative. (More in Step Three.) What is his self-image, and how far off reality is it? What are his likes and dislikes?

How do we come by this kind of information? In some cases, from direct experience and observation. In other instances, from background information that we obtain from other persons or from written sources. And, whether we intend to do so or not, we will be forming, intuitively, a picture of the other person from the time we make an appointment or bump into him on the street until our next encounter or episode. Sometimes, one of our most difficult problems is trying to erase first, or early, impressions.

With settings and conditions, as with persons, you prepare at the general level and at the specific level. At the general level, for example, you know that a good meal generally sets the stage for good conversation. But can you be sure that the meal will be a "good" meal? Or, you know that a lesson plan you've used in the past generally is a good approach. But you cannot be sure this plan will work in *this* situation.

Moving from the general to the specific, several approaches are available to you regarding situations. In any event, you will try to differentiate between the current situation and other situations with which you are familiar. You will prepare for these variations insofar as you can "read" them. You may try to control the situation, holding the variations to a minimum, so that you will be operating under circumstances with which you feel comfortable. We do this when our repertoire is limited; sometimes it works, sometimes it doesn't.

Or, you can prepare the best you can, then remain open and flexible, ready to deal with contingencies as they arise. This is, of course, the best approach. (You will learn more about "reading" a situation in Step Three.)

Your planning for a communication event (be it a banquet or a heart-to-heart talk with a friend) is in some ways similar to a coach's preparation for a football game.

As a coach, you've studied football as a sport, an art, a science. Your preparation may have begun back when you were a kid, but as a professional, you have become expert in the principles and the rules.

These men are yours to mold into a fighting machine. You direct the development of their bodies. You study each man's skills and place him strategically. You lay your game plan.

You recognize that you will not be able to control all the eventualities, such as Jonesey turning into the King of Fumbles or Smitty's being benched by an old injury. But you can control the preparation. You can set your goals in keeping with your purpose and objectives. You can evaluate your own resources and the resources of the opposition. You can have a Plan A, even a Plan Z. To a degree, you can test these plans, both theoretically and in practice sessions.

When the players charge out of the locker room, you sense that this is it. But you do not resign yourself to Fate. You remain tuned to the game as it unfolds, and

Step One: Prepare

you cope with contingencies as they arise.

It's like this in other life situations that depend heavily upon successful communication. Take, for example, the case of a man who needs to win a job. Picture yourself as the applicant. Let's say that the job you want to land is commensurate with your purpose, objectives, interests, and resources. Through education and training, you have prepared yourself. You consider yourself qualified.

But you cannot, as if by magic, transmit your assurance to the interviewer, nor will you be able to control the interview or anticipate all of the eventualities.

You can prepare, however, and so you formulate your "game" plan. You run through your role mentally in a sort of skull practice; you rehearse possible responses in a sort of scrimmage. You may confide in a family member or friend.

There are so many variables! What kind of person will be the interviewer? Will you be able to "read" him? What image should you project?

Should you come on strong — or might the interviewer judge you brash?

How should you dress? Your clothing will communicate. You wouldn't go to an interview for a job as teller in a conservative bank wearing the same kind of outfit you'd wear if you were seeking a job as public relations man for a baseball team.

How much personal information will you reveal? Will the interviewer warm to your efforts in the area of social reform? Does mention of this vital aspect of your life pose too great a risk? Sooner or later, the employer is bound to learn — but do you wait until you get to know each other, providing a base for understanding?

You don't always have the opportunity to be so deliberate in planning for communication experiences. Say you have just received a telephone message that a neighbor's son has been killed in an automobile wreck. You've been asked to go over and notify the neighbor.

How does one communicate a death message? In this excruciating moment, you'd like to know how other messengers have managed. But there is no time for that. In a minute or two, you are going to have to go next door and say — what? You have no time to prepare, but you feel that you must get your wits about you. This is a task for a clergyman or policeman, not an assignment for a layman — or is it? You wish you had a minister — someone — to go with you.

Will you tell the neighbor the news straight out? Or will you introduce it by saying, "There's been an accident. Your son was involved." How do you move from there? Maybe you ought to prepare yourself in prayer?

Fortunately, not all of life's communication efforts are so earnest as this one. And you usually have more time to prepare. But *all* communication is important, and you don't take someone to lunch or even share a coffee break with a person without a minute amount of preparation — each involves at least one decision made against alternatives. And, really, you never know just how much importance attaches to a greeting or a pat on the back. How frequently, when someone receives word of a suicide, remorse sweeps over him. "If I had just known that he was depressed, I could have . . ."

In real life, every drama — whether tragedy or comedy — is important. And, for every drama, the stage has to

Step One: Prepare 17

be set properly. Life is on stage every moment of the day and night. You have to decide what your role will be; you have to communicate *yourself* to the rest of the world.

You have to prepare. You build the walls of your castle and cap them off with a roof. But even as you are building, you invite other persons to cross over the bridge and visit with you. And you take time out to visit with them.

To build a castle and to become a good host or guest — both take preparation. Your decisions are the blocks for your castle; their validity will determine how strong the castle will be. Similarly, your effectiveness as a communicator will be determined by the aggregate of your successes and failures and how you react to them.

Your best laid plans may not work — not the first time, maybe not the second or third time. They may be "good" plans, but they just aren't right for the particular person or group, for this moment in time. But your efforts will not have been wasted if you will seize upon the episode and turn it into a learning experience. You sometimes learn more from failure than from success. So keep your eye on the "radar screen" of life, noting the blips, and using them as guides for changing your course.

Communication is both an art and a science, a mixture of common sense expressions and carefully honed expressions. Communication can be tearfully touching, uproariously funny, or calculatedly cold. Your preparation for person-to-person communication must include an understanding of the variety and power inherent in the process. Apply this understanding to add variety and value toward your interface with other people.

The trick is to have *form* follow *function*, rather than the other way around. The medium is dictated by the message. A minister may be a good communicator; a professor may be a good communicator; a PR man may be a good communicator — in their respective bailiwicks. But these same individuals may or may not be good communicators at the breakfast table or in the bedroom. Could their failure owe to their not taking their *domestic* communicating as seriously as they take their *professional* communicating? Could it be that they don't prepare for communicating with their families?

How seriously do you take communicating with your family, business associates, friends, casual acquaintances?

Your communicating will be no better than your preparation, and your preparation will be no better than the values you assign to yourself and to other human beings. The Golden Rule of communication is, "Say unto others as you would have them to say unto you," and "Listen to others as you would have them listen to you."

Do you understand "people"? Do you take the time and effort to get to know *persons*? Are you willing to accept the person where he is now? You have a good basis for caring. After all, this other person is, like you, a child of God. That makes him your brother! And that makes him pretty important!

You have reason to care. And if you *care*, you will *prepare*!

Step One: Prepare

For Your Practice

The exercises which appear here and at the end of each subsequent chapter are an essential part of your "seven steps." Taking them seriously will insure that you appropriate the material into your own everyday living. Keeping a notebook can be helpful; in it, you can record the results of the exercises described here, plus the results of independent studies and observations.

1. In your place of work, or while you are shopping or attending a meeting, study the people around you and ask yourself, "On the basis of what I observe, would I hire this person?" Make a mental or written checklist of the characteristics that would affect your choice, ranking them in descending order of importance.

2. Now reflect upon characteristics of your own which would recommend you to a prospective employer. Jot down these attributes. How well do you measure up? Go back to Exercise 1, above. Do you care to assign a different ranking to any of those characteristics?

2. Using your list of personal characteristics (2 above), make an inventory of your weak points. Now, during the next 24-hour period, engage in a concerted effort to improve your position.

4. Choose a goal that you would like to promote with a member of your family, an associate at work, a friend, a group. Ideally, this would be something you've thought of suggesting for a long time. Before you adopt this goal as the one you will pursue, however, check it against (a) your purpose and your objectives, and (b) your interests and resources.

If the goal still seems appropriate, prepare to "sell" it as a professional salesman might go about selling a big order of goods. Study your "prospect," his/her personality, motivations, needs, etc. Familiarize yourself with your goal in detail. Why should your "prospect" be interested in helping you to obtain this goal? How will you get this person to let down his drawbridge so that you can come over and communicate with him?

Now that you've gone to this much effort, why not put your planning into practice?

5. Select an occasion or arrange a situation when you will be alone with someone who is important to you. The occasion may be a date, conference, or a chat after a meal, etc. Open your conversation with a topic that you know to be important to the *other* person. Ask questions that will draw out his interests, questions "how to" and "why." Sustain this topic for five or ten minutes or longer. Afterward, reflect on whether or not the "you" approach strengthened (a) your conversation, and (b) your relationship.

6. In 5, above, did you feel uncomfortable devoting so much time and attention to the *other person*? Did he attempt to have you let down *your* "drawbridge" so that he could visit *you* in *your* "castle"? Over the years, have you been too much a "listen to me!" type — or do you think that you often don't come on strong enough, thereby forfeiting opportunities to share of yourself?

7. On your next grocery-shopping outing (and if there isn't to be a "next one," plan one), take your planning seriously and see if planning makes a difference. As you do your shopping, reflect upon the interpersonal implications of what you buy. To what extent is your

Step One: Prepare 21

shopping affected by the likes or dislikes of other persons? (As to the kinds of things you buy, brands, quantities, variety, etc.) Is grocery shopping a type of communication?

8. Make a list of other "routine" tasks (additional to grocery shopping) which have a communication content. Would you enjoy these tasks more (or at least *tolerate* them better) if you acknowledged to yourself the communication element that's in them?

STEP 2 LISTEN

To listen is
  . to be still
  . to expect
  . to wait for a response
  . to practice restraint.

In a book entitled *Talk That Gets Results* (McGraw Hill, New York, 1957), K. C. Ingram shares these valuable observations:

> In a conference or in a conversation with another person there appears to be unanimous agreement among communication specialists that a person's personal interests are best served by being a good listener, or an open minded listener. (Page 54)

Step Two: Listen

We have to risk having our own minds changed in discussion with people or we won't learn much. And certainly we won't win the cooperation that is necessary for success in industrial, professional or social life unless we learn to listen. (Page 130)

The biggest block to personal communication is man's inability to listen intelligently, understandingly, and skillfully to another person. (Page 131)

Hearing is the "mechanical" process by which sound is perceived. There is a difference between *hearing* and *listening*. Listening is more sophisticated; it requires giving attention, interpreting, understanding. Listening requires discipline. You have to block out — or filter out — extraneous sounds and irrelevant thoughts. As you are listening, you are assigning weight to the components of what you hear and you are considering what response you will make. Just to decide whether to remain silent or to make an overt response can be crucial.

Why listen? Here are some reasons:

1. You gain new information. Through the information transfer process, you add to the inventory of your knowledge warehouse. Thus, by listening, one gains an education.

2. You share. The other person listens to your problems, interests, achievements, and you listen to his. In this way, you reaffirm and support each other.

3. You gain self-fulfillment. Many people will willingly tell you how they have made money, gained better

health, or found peace of mind. You will catch visions, sharpen goals, learn how to lay plans of action; you may find the key to successful living.

4. You obtain an understanding of how much, or how little, the other person knows. You will get a reading of his knowledge; thereby, you will become able to evaluate his competence in a given area — to judge how much stock to put in him along this line. Also, you will discern the level at which to respond when your time to speak comes. By listening, a good teacher is able to "peg" a student, avoiding the possibility of either talking down to him or talking over his head. Beside, it's a big waste and bother for someone to try to teach you something you already know.

5. You will recognize when you should punch your "action" button and when you should refrain from action.

6. You will learn how to persuade — to convince people of the merits of your proposals and to enlist them in your cause.

You will notice that I didn't say listening is the quickest, easiest, or best way to gain knowledge or insights. However, under given circumstances, listening may deserve those superlatives. But I think we're glib enough about listening; we've been doing it all our lives and we assume that we're pretty good at it, when, in fact, few of us *are* good at listening.

True listening isn't easy. In the first place, opting to listen rather than to express requires sensitivity and discipline. Secondly, true listening requires concentration, which can be draining. Much, of course, depends

Step Two: Listen

on the person who is doing the listening (and the person who is speaking, obviously). A visually oriented person might obtain information more rapidly, and with better comprehension, by watching or reading.

But listening has a number of advantages over other methods. It affords intimacy — you are there. You have a front seat when the emotional dramas of life are acted out; you catch the tonal qualities and inflections of voice, for example.

The sensitive person is always reading the emotional wave length of expressions as well as the "dictionary" content of words themselves. In the following pairs of quotations, note the implications of emotion which I have tried to convey even though I am limited to the use of black marks on white paper:

"If you would only stop talking and listen, you might know what is happening." She twisted a button on her red jacket, her pointed chin quivering.

"If you would only stop talking and listen, you might know what is happening." She giggled and threw her arms around him.

"Please listen to me. I need your help." Karen, supervisor of The Suicide Prevention Center, gripped the telephone as she responded to the desperate man's voice.

"Please listen to me. I need your help." He smiled that half-shy, half-pleading way that had made him the best salesman in the company.

"Please let me tell my side of the story," Arn chortled, aiming an elaborate wink at his wife.

"Please let me tell my side of the story." Her frail ten-year-old body was rigid and her gray eyes sparkled with unshed tears.

Let's look at other advantages that listening affords in comparison with other methods:

1. The spoken word is the quickest method for disseminating news bulletins, whether by commercial medium or an individual; it follows, therefore, that listening is the quickest method for receiving such news. (Presuming that you are awake and available to hear at the time the news is conveyed.)

2. Talk-and-listen permits reciprocation. "Mother-in-law" and "wife" jokes to the contrary, it is a back-and-forth method, providing maximal opportunity for personal sharing. A related advantage is flexibility — there can be gradual or radical shifts in positions and agendas.

3. Under some conditions, listening may be the *only* way to assimilate information of an order beyond rudimentary impressions. Talking books for the blind, for example. Or listening to a taped lecture while driving a car. Listening can dispel loneliness and relieve monotony.

4. Under the right circumstances, listening can be the best of methods. It can be so entertaining as to seem effortless. For certain types of data, listening (especially when combined with visual reception) affords maximum retention.

Knowing when to talk and when to listen — being able to achieve the proper mix of talking and listening —

Step Two: Listen

knowing when to utilize other methods — these are some of the essential elements of becoming an effective communicator.

Because of its possibilities for back-and-forth exchanges, the talk-listen-talk method can be immensely creative. Join me in some arithmetic games:

A child is taught that 1 + 1 = 2. This is true in "numbers" arithmetic, but it can be untrue in "people" arithmetic. If two people are supposed to be communicating with each other and one cops out, you have nothing. The noncommunicating person has set up a block.

Notice this couple: They have lived together for years. The husband repeats the same old stories and the wife automatically gives him the responses that he needs to keep going. One track of her mental process is geared to his presence; meanwhile, she uses her other tracks for her own purposes. Since she isn't listening, one and one equal not two, but zero.

On the other hand, one and one may equal something beyond two. When you declare ideas that interest me, I develop my own ideas to match yours. Together, we create new ideas. There is a new dimension — multiplication. Perhaps a process that has been working in my mind has also been at work in yours. Your ideas and mine give rise to composite ideas. And in the back-and-forth of communication, refinements are made, and manifold ideas emerge.

The watchword is to keep addition and multiplication at work, and to avoid subtraction.

While we're discussing numbers, I'll share with you the observation that groups of three tend to be less productive than two persons or four or more persons. Research by experts corroborates this rather obvious phenomenon. (Mothers have observed since the beginning of time that when a third child comes over, trouble begins. Likewise with romantic triangles.) The reason for the difficulty isn't precisely clear, but probably lies in the inability of a group to maintain absolute balance in its interactions. When four or more persons are present, imbalances are less obvious, and they are more easily tolerated if they are noted. Keep in mind that the experts define a "small group" as numbering four to twenty-five persons. This doesn't mean that you should, at all costs, avoid threesomes; rather, you should be sensitive to the dynamics of threesomes. Work hard to see that nobody feels left out and be wary of aligning yourself with either party.

Because listening is so productive of material achievements and life-enriching experience, I would like to share with you a system for listening and for retaining what was said. Although I've forgotten the source, I remember the substance of the "ACE Memory Training System."

The system is built upon three basic words:

A — Attention

C — Concentration

E — Expression

Attention: This is the process of directing your faculties on an object or a person.

How many times, upon being introduced to someone, have you failed to get his name straight? Or dismissed his name as unimportant? But then you found a need to recall his name — perhaps to introduce him to someone,

Step Two: Listen

or to get in touch with him at a later date. (It's embarrassing to chat with a person before dinner, then find yourself seated next to him and be unable to introduce him to acquaintances about you!)

A person's name is a sweet sound to him, so why forfeit the opportunity to get off to a good start? Latch onto his name. Listen when he says it. If you don't quite get it, ask him to repeat it. If it appears that your relationship will be more than a casual one, ask if he has a card. (You might offer your own card, if you have one.) Even if you should subsequently forget his name, he will nonetheless appreciate the importance that you attached to it.

Concentration: This is the process of focusing all your faculties, *intensely* and *deeply*, upon a person or thing.

A good relationship with a person depends upon your showing that you consider him important. Look him in the eye, give him a firm handshake, speak directly to him — *don't* treat him in a nonchalant and offhanded manner.

You cannot *sustain* interest in a person unless you have learned something about him. Moreover, you cannot sustain interest even after you have learned something about him unless you uncover at least one characteristic that you admire or respect.

Your respect is dependent upon your *listening*, and your listening is dependent upon your respecting him. This means that you have to draw the person out, which may not be easy. If he is reticent, you do not wish to invade his privacy, so you move adroitly — to use boxing terminology, you employ footwork. You may have to shift your approach again and again. Also, you will have to be sensitive to the *real* meaning of what he seems to be saying.

Expression: By either writing down the information, or using it orally, you engrave it in your mind.

Let's say that you concentrated on the name of a woman upon being introduced to her. You've got it, but will you have it for long? To burn the name into your memory, *express* it! Express it several times: "I'm pleased to meet you, Mrs. *Throgmorton.* We have a Mr. John *Throgmorton* in our plant. Could it be that you are related? . . . It was nice meeting you, Mrs. *Throgmorton.*" If it's especially important that you retain the name, jot it down.

This, then, is the ACE Memory Training System. To recap: You focus your faculties on the subject, person, name, etc. You concentrate. You reinforce your power of recall by expressing the name, etc. Meanwhile, you command your mind — you program it — to remember.

One method of programming is association. Memory experts perform astounding feats of memory — for example, they recall, in proper order, a list of one hundred or more items called out to them in rapid-fire succession. Some of the experts use a "master" code — for example, instead of "1" the person thinks "table," and when item No. 1 is sounded, he speedily pictures this item *resting on a table.* If the item is alligator, he visualizes an alligator on a table — which isn't hard to recall, is it? But be forewarned, systems of association are fraught with peril. There was the minister who was developing his power of recall, using the association method. He met a Mrs. Orb. Noting that she had big

Step Two: Listen

eyes, he related "Orb" and "eye." Alas! the next time he met Mrs. Orb, he greeted her with, "Hello there, Mrs. Goggle."

The ACE system and similar systems are so simple that some persons scoff at them. Salting one's food is a simple process, too. But the simplicity doesn't deter us from seasoning our food.

The intense attention, concentration, and expression that characterize the relationship of sweethearts are not inherent in many other relationships. For sweethearts, listening may come effortlessly, but it may not be so easy for a boss to listen to a disgruntled employee or a householder to listen to his garrulous neighbor. Communication is a two-way street, and when the traffic is moving smoothly and you're getting somewhere, it's wonderful. But there are obstacles that make communication tentative or shallow, or cut off the flow entirely. I call these curbs "the three Busy B's." They are: *Blocks, Barriers,* and *Bars*. The Busy B's will get you if you don't watch out.

We'll be talking about the Busy B's throughout this book, but for now, let's look at a couple of kinds of barriers that interfere with listening: (1) an *inability* to listen — really listen, and (2) an *unwillingness* to listen (which is to say, ignoring the other person's right to express himself and to be heard).

Because conditioned responses and willful responses are divided by a very thin line, it isn't easy to diagnose a case of poor listening. Failure to listen can arise out of an impulsive nature, selfishness, emotional upset, bad habits, a lack of appreciation for the benefits of listening, or a lack of listening skills. The important thing, however, is to recognize that you can be a better listener than you are. First, you come to know your own personality, your own ways of reacting. Then, you discover the best ways for you to overcome your problems. Finally, you keep working at improvement — overcoming difficulties of long standing takes time.

Passions and prejudices can tune out what's being said. Racial prejudice, for example. The fact that a person is black or white becomes more important than what he's trying to communicate.

Anger interferes with listening. Many a child has been punished wrongly because a parent couldn't or didn't control his emotions long enough to hear the child's explanation. If a wife is overcome with anger, her husband can talk until he is blue in the face and she won't hear him.

Injured feelings plug one's ears. Say that your best friend gives a party and you don't receive an invitation. She explains that there must have been a mail failure, or that she wasn't able to get you on the phone, but you don't really hear her because of your disappointment or lingering doubts.

You don't listen well when you're anxious. A physician may meticulously spell out instructions for taking a prescribed drug, but if you are concerned about your condition, you may not remember a thing he said.

When you're uptight, that's precisely the time when you most need to listen! Be sensitive to your inner situation; recognize occasions when your emotions are rendering you deaf to what the other person is trying to say.

Step Two: Listen

As you listen, remember that the words can be 180 degrees from the true direction of a person's feelings. For example, he may speak with contrived diffidence when, actually, his heart is about to break. A bland remark may be a disguised cry for help; a defiant stance may cover up a longing to be loved. Sometimes a reading of the tone of voice or body language discovers the real message.

"John, what do you want for dinner tonight?"

You're tired and all day you've longed for your slippers and comfortable chair in front of the TV. But your wife's tone says, "Show some appreciation and attention."

"I've been craving some Mexican food," you lie. (Surely, God will forgive such a gentle evasion of the truth.) "Let's dress up and go out to eat."

(Step Three is "Read," and in that chapter, we'll go more deeply into the art of interpreting real meanings as they may be discovered in inflections of voice, body language, group interactions, etc.)

While I don't want to let poor listeners off the hook, I do want to acknowledge my sympathy for them. In our modern age, listening has fallen upon hard times. Early man used the two ears that God has given us — if he didn't he perished. Fortunately for our ancestors, they were trained to use their ears; besides, they lived is a hushed world.

But today we are not encouraged to listen. Oh, our parents *demand* that we listen, but often this sets up an emotional block. Certainly, few parents set an example (which is the highest type of teaching) by listening to their children. Little children are endowed with a sense of wonder, but our practical-minded adult society soon squeezes that out of them. We should, instead, encourage the child to listen in on the magical sounds of the universe, including human voices.

Nor does our educational system encourage listening, although it's built on a lecture base. It's the business of the teacher to educate you, but, really, a person cannot be stuffed with education. You learn by hitting upon the right questions, searching until you find the answers, and concentrating until you master the method or subject matter. Ideally, the process takes place under the guidance and direction of a challenging and understanding mentor. What I'm saying is that if you want to learn, you must first learn to listen.

There are a couple of other reasons why so many of us don't listen well. One reason is that we are under relentless pressures, among them pressures of deadlines, travel, status, etc. Another reason is, we're bombarded by all sorts of irrelevant noises.

We moderns are immersed in noise — the throbbing of engines, the shrieking of sirens, the blaring of hi-fi's, the authoritarian calling of intercoms. Indeed, we are so accustomed to noise that an acoustically dead building drives us silly; we even go so far as to install a device which emits a low hum.

Whether noisy living is going to do serious long-range harm to man (individual or species), is still being argued by the experts. Some say that the generation of the last two decades will have forfeited acuteness of hearing to loud noises, including rock music. I would suggest that turning up the volume not only deafens ears, but also damages other parts of the nervous system, as well. Man

Step Two: Listen

has a marvelous reserve of mind, body, and spirit, but there is a limit to the overloading that he can tolerate.

The best conversations are painted upon either a white canvas of silence, or over a pastel background of soothing sounds. Prepare for conversations by seeking out settings that are conducive to good listening. Then insure communication by offering the other person generous portions of silence. The idea is for the two of you (or the group) to work together at building conversation. It's defeating to try to work around the fringes of invading noises or to compete in one-upmanship.

Try substituting appreciative silence, accompanied by a warm smile or an affirming nod, for cutting words. And when you aren't sure what your response should be, insert silence. "When in doubt, leave it out." Think how much better the world would be if some of its leaders practiced silence and listening instead of filling the void with idle words.

Work at the art of listening and the rewards will more than compensate you for the considerable time and effort that improvement requires.

Listen, and for *practical* reasons — to improve your economic or social position. Even look at it in this crass way: When you've got to spend time with people (regardless), why waste this time and forfeit possible benefits by either shutting your ears or half-listening?

Listen, and for *humanitarian* reasons. There are untold millions of persons in the world who hunger for one thing more than anything else, and that is for an attentive and sympathetic ear. Not for someone to tell them what to do, mind you, but simply to hear them out.

We're conditioned to believe that we have to *say* something or *do* something if we are to be helpful. We can help by listening.

An internist had given his hospitalized patient several thorough physicals and had subjected her to numerous x-ray checks and laboratory tests. He could find no indication of a physical abnormality.

It happened that as he was leaving her room, he bumped into a psychiatrist-friend in the hallway. "Bill," he said, "I'd certainly appreciate it if you'd have a look at Mrs. Jones in 306. She's practically incapacitated with vague complaints, but I can't spot her problem."

The psychiatrist went in, introduced himself by name, commented that "I understand you've been having some trouble," pulled up a chair — and began listening. He listened for an hour, and during this time his only utterances were protests that he really must be going.

Next day, the psychiatrist and internist encountered each other and the internist said, "Bill, Mrs. Jones insists that she's able to go home today, thanks to you. *Whatever did you say to that lady?*"

Listen, and for *spiritual* reasons. "Be still, and know that I am God." If you happen to be a person who is devoted to humanism, as contrasted with religion, I appeal to you, be still and listen to your conscience. (I believe that while you are still, and open, God will communicate with you.)

Step Two: Listen

For Your Practice

1. Give yourself a listening test. During the course of a day or evening, see how many times you say things like:
"Huh?"
"What was it you said?"
"Sorry, but I didn't hear you."
"I'm afraid I wasn't listening closely."
"Do what? Go where?"
"Why didn't you tell me?"
If you wind up with a clean slate, sell this book. If you sinned one to three times, prepare to work harder at your listening. If you erred more than three times, see if you need a hearing aid.

2. If a tape recorder is available to you, record a conversation with a family member or friend. As a matter of courtesy, let him/her know that you are recording your conversation, but do not specify the reason, or artificiality may result. Choose a subject that holds enthusiastic interest for both of you. Later, replay the tape and listen for instances in which you interrupted, indicated that you weren't listening, or evidenced other bad habits identified in this chapter.

Rate your listening ability: poor, fair, good, or excellent. If you are keeping a notebook, enter your score. Upon completing this course, check yourself for improvement.

3. For a meeting or interview, have a notebook or pad handy. Instead of interrupting the other person(s) to express your questions or comments, jot them down.

Then, when the other person indicates he's through speaking, offer your questions or comments.

Observe how helpful this device can be — how much more polite, how economical of time and energy.

Later, reflect on these questions: Would you have gained anything by butting in? Did you find that the other person sometimes answered your question without your having to ask it? Did your jotting down a question or comment give you time to evaluate it and figure the best way to express it?

4. On an occasion when you have called a meeting or requested an interview (or when you are presiding), have a pad handy and jot down key words which reflect what the other person(s) said. At the conclusion of the session, offer a brief summary of what was said (and accomplished, if that's appropriate). You may also ask for clarification, definitive action, etc. Afterward, evaluate the method.

5. The next time you are introduced to someone, put the ACE memory technique into action. See if it works.

6. You may want to check a library for articles and books on listening and on memory development.

7. Think back on a conversation in which you participated today or yesterday. In retrospect, do you feel it would have been better for you to have (a) come on stronger, or (b) been quieter? Recall from experience an occasion where you should have come on strong but didn't. Recall also when you should have exercised restraint but didn't. What were the results?

8. In some families, peace is maintained by one person avoiding conversation with another member. Is it ever like this in your home? If so, are you the person

Step Two: Listen 39

avoided? Or, do you do the avoiding? Read the following six items. (If your family happens to be a "problem" family, anchor these points in your mind.)

    (a) Recognize that you are probably deficient in the art of listening.

    (b) Determine that you are going to develop the skill of listening, and practice the art until you are proficient.

    (c) Set a definite goal to be quiet at appropriate times. Learn to subdue the urge to interrupt; wait until the other person has made his pitch and the time is right for you to make your contribution.

    (d) Learn to ask pertinent questions. Give the other person the respect of your full attention when you have requested information.

    (e) Always remember that you do not know everything about everything.

    (f) Be willing to be "little i," meanwhile casting the other person in the role of "Big U."

9. In your next interpersonal encounter, concentrate on the following:

    (a) the other person's importance

    (b) the need for allowing the other person to become himself

    (c) by listening, you increase your own effectiveness.

10. Approach the next sermon by your minister, speech by your boss, conference with a business associate, address at your club, etc., with a renewed commitment to get the most out of what's said. Listen with "new" ears. Listen to the major points and the phrasing. Ap-

propriate for later use some apt expression or powerful thought. Afterwards, recap in your mind the theme and the essentials. Use one or more of the materials in conversation.

STEP 3 "READ"

"Read." Sure, you know what that word means. But let's give "read" extra breadth and depth. Let's let "read" mean
- . to observe
- . to become aware
- . to be percipient
- . to assess.

Whatever connotation you place upon this verb, reading is an essential activity in our lives. You can't get through a day without reading something — newspaper, grocery list, instructions, street signs. And "reading," when it means to be percipient, can be important, too. Just ask the husband who has failed to "read" his wife's mood. (And this goes for wives who don't "read" their husbands, and for any of hundreds of other kinds of relationships.)

If a husband or a wife emits a peculiar little sound, the spouse had better run up the antennae and "read" what's going on. Better to "read" an early signal than to have to listen to the full message later.

The setting: Place, a home. Time, end of a rainy work day. Enter John, who has had a bad day at the shop.

"Why can't you try to get home on time?" Mary cries. "The roast is ruined by now!"

John prudently holds his tongue. He sizes up the situation that has made his normally cheerful wife edgy. Their cozy little cottage is littered with toys. Their four lively youngsters have spent the day indoors sandpapering his wife's nerves.

"This storm has given you a rougher day than even I had, Mary. I finished that Williston order and left the shop in time, but the Fourth Street viaduct was flooded. Detouring cost me thirty minutes. I'm sorry I'm late. Nobody hates dry roast more than I do."

Mary smiles. "Maybe a little extra ketchup will fix it up."

"I'll help the kids gather up all these toys right after dinner."

Smart boy!

He that hath ears to hear, let him hear! To which we can add: *He that hath faculties to "hear," let him "hear."*

Remember that most of the meaning in a communication process, as with most of the ice in an iceberg, can be under the surface and hidden from view. The obscured meaning can be sighted only with inner vision.

Step Three: "Read"

And only by seeing the part which isn't apparent will you know when to respond and when to be silent, what to contribute and what to withhold. So, it's well worth your while to study yourself and your fellow human beings in order to understand the way we tick.

Although it's a vast oversimplification, we can compare our minds to tape player-recorders. Our tape player may be a monaural, a two-track, or eight-track machine. Similarly, our minds can be single-track or multi-track. Except that in the case of our minds, the reference to number of tracks applies to the way we use them rather than to their manufacture.

It's possible for us to have more than one track of our minds going at a given time. Consider, for example, two people traveling through the countryside. One is a professional conservationist. He is driving the car, and he's using one track (at least *part* of a track, we hope) for decisions concerning the road. Meanwhile, he's devoting another track to conversation with his companion concerning a hobby in which they have a shared interest. At the same time, the conservationist has yet another track "reading" the land, its features, and the uses to which the land is being put.

Our minds are like complex instruments for simultaneously recording many aspects of the weather — temperature, humidity, barometric pressure, etc. Except that our mental and emotional processes are infinitely more complex. It is even an insult to their complexity to compare them to a computer.

To continue the tape-player analogy, some of our tracks can be in operation without our being conscious of it. A finger touches a hot stove and is retracted before we become consciously aware of either the hazard or the hurt.

All tracks are busily imprinting their impressions, occasionally pausing to replay an experience. Again, the replay may come from the tape library deep within our subconscious. We may not be able to hear the recording clearly; its significance may be vague and confusing. A whiff of a certain perfume, for example, may replay a memory so dimmed by time that we experience only vague feelings of pleasure, or uneasiness.

Our "computer" integrates the impulses from all of our various tracks. The computer permits our lives to be the sum total of all our experiences: what happened in the past and what is happening now, plus our anticipation of (or concern for) the future.

It is the integration of the tracks and the interpretation of their data which permits us to "read" our situation, to plan, and to spot trouble and begin taking steps either to avoid it or to minimize its effect. A good "reader" can detect turbulence in a person or group, and, by evaluating all the data, decide whether a storm is impending. For example, by reading body language, he may see that his audience is getting edgy during his speech, or see that in a buzz group, "A" is becoming annoyed with "B."

Reading the nudge of the subconscious can be a life-saving habit. Just five days before the writing of this page, while driving my car, I had an intuitive feeling of approaching danger. I slowed down. I can't explain my impulse to brake the car, but I'm thankful that I did. An approaching car passed a truck and missed my car by a few inches. Lives were spared because I

Step Three: "Read"

obeyed the silent voice of my subconscious.

The person with a highly developed and alert "reading" mechanism has a distinct advantage in communication.

Let's say that you are such a person and you are attending a town meeting to support plans for a low-rent housing complex. Earlier, you have picked up rumblings of opposition, but you don't have a reliable feeling for the balance of power.

You begin "reading" the meeting. You note that as the people gather, they do not mix freely; instead, they cluster. Their eyes dart about the room. They, too, are reading. They call one another's attention to the constituency of other clusters, and animated conversation follows. From your own reading of the clusters, you recognize that some groups are "conservative" and some are "liberal."

The chairman has difficulty getting the meeting to order. As he states the call of the meeting, you read his own opposition. While the leading proponent of the housing development tries to explain the plan, there is a great deal of throat-clearing and enough muttering to be distracting. Then, when those in opposition are invited to voice their views, you are surprised to find among them many whom you had assessed as being with you. Still others whom you thought to be in your camp are expressing ambivalence.

Meantime, your "computer" is whirring away, mixing "intensity" data with "numbers" data. You finger the "print-out" and see that the chances for approval at this meeting are slim. On this basis, you suggest that a vote be delayed until additional information can be obtained and more time allotted for discussion.

"Mr. Jones has made a motion that the proposal be tabled," the chairman says.

You quickly read his intent — he is pushing you into a sticky position, technically. He isn't echoing your motion; he's out to kill the proposal.

"No, Mr. Chairman. My motion is not to *table*, but merely to postpone a vote."

Your motion carries. You have lost a battle, but you have avoided a prompt and demoralizing defeat. Your side will have a chance to pull back and regroup, and to revise its strategy.

In your communication experiences, develop a facility for reading

- what is being said
- how it is being said
- who is saying it
- what is not being said
- what is intended but not verbalized
- body language
- group interplay (if you're in a group)
- movement, and its direction and momentum
- how the pieces fit into the "big picture."

To be perceptive demands the use of our "outer" senses combined with our "inner" sense. As in the following example:

"Daddy! Daddy!" You hear the desperate voice of your youngest child. "Mr. Jones is killing Fluff!"

Your immediate reaction is to fly to the defense of that furry member of your family. You want to grab up some weapon and lay Jones low among his sweet peas. But as you interpret the torrent of words, caution damps

Step Three: "Read" 47

your anger. You know Mr. Jones is no fiend (even if he is a bit weird); also, you know that every young child tends to exaggerate at times. The tone of Junior's voice suggests a lack of objectivity.

A quick look out the window confirms your suspicions. Jerry Jones has shooed your cat out of his sweet pea bed again. Already she's perched on top of your car, treating herself to a luxurious spit bath.

Every situation is different and every person is different; moreover, situations and persons are dynamic. They're forever shifting. The trick is to understand *people generally* (to understand human nature); beyond this, to be able to read *individuals*, and, further, to be able to read the individual's *mood*. It follows that you should acquire an understanding of group interactions generally and, beyond this, develop the ability to read a particular group and its current mood. Only by reading a person or group can you (1) prepare for a communication experience, (2) make adjustments as you go, and (3) arrive at real sharing.

Let's look for a moment at the different kinds of "mind sets" that we find in people. Although I acknowledge that any generalization I send up can be shot full of holes with exceptions, I would like to describe three "sets" of mind:

The open mind. The person with this set of mind finds excitement and challenge in exposure to new stimuli. He possesses a "want to" spirit, is eager to learn. He can deal with change without feeling seriously threatened.

This doesn't mean that the open-minded person won't present problems; he will. He may be so open-minded that he will accept anything and everything; because of his enthusiasm, he may tend to bite off more than he can chew. He may lack holding power — he may flash and then fizzle out. But at least he's accessible!

The closed mind. This person tells himself: "They can't tell me anything. I know more than they do; I haven't time to waste on them." Or, "They won't pay any attention to what I think, anyhow. Besides, what difference will this project (or whatever) make?" This person will point out flaws in people and proposals even before he becomes acquainted with them. He begins objecting before he has heard the goal of a campaign, the text of a proposal. Often he is a source of noise and discord; he takes discussions sideways and backward, not forward.

Often, a person with a closed mind wants to boss other people and impress them with his own importance. He does not want his prejudices disturbed.

Don't write off everyone who happens to have a "closed" mind, however. There are too many of them for them to be dismissed; sometimes their approval or acquiescence is essential. Often, you find persons with a closed mind set entrenched in the power structure, having gotten there by their single-mindedness of purpose and their compulsive drive.
or two!")

Besides, it won't do for us to be closed-minded about our open-mindedness. Each of us has some closed corners in his mind.

You approach the person with the closed mind by appealing to an area where he feels competent or otherwise secure. You may compliment him on a piece of

Step Three: "Read"

work well done. Bulwarking his self-image is a fairly sure way to get him to let down his drawbridge.

The tentative mind. He won't say "yes" and he won't say "no." Even a "maybe" comes hard. He wants to learn *all* the facts, and to test them. It is hard for him to make up his mind, determine his own response.

This person can't afford to fail, for his self-image requires perfection. He has many warriors armed with "if's" guarding his castle. Why is he so cautious? He has probably been "shot down" many times. He doesn't want to be the target again. Like the closed-minded person, he needs self-assurance.

We're each a mix. We are open-minded in some areas, closed in others, tentative in still others. We're a part of all that we have met, including our won-and-lost record and how we feel about that record. Anyone can use a little reassurance — yet, it's important to recognize that some persons are either too "hard" or too self-effacing to sit still for very much reassuring.

Whatever the type, accept him where he is. Convince him that you regard him as a person of value. Show him the mutuality of your interests. Share with him your purpose, objectives, goals, and your plan. Be ready to volunteer, or to acknowledge, the good as well as the bad points. (Sometimes you take the wind out of a critic's sails by openly pointing to flaws or drawbacks in your proposals.)

Stop, look, listen, read. What does this person (this group) *really* feel? What is he (the group) *really* saying?

If, at an annual meeting, the chairman of the board talks of an obvious fiasco in terms of its beneficial aspects, you can read that he is sensitive about this reversal. Perhaps you should be alert to the possibility of further repercussions within the organization.

That little laugh. Does it reflect humor — or hurt? That comment. It seems to be in opposition to your proposal — but was opposition the intention of the speaker, or was he merely clumsy with his words? (Perhaps you'd better ask for clarification, or act on the assumption that he's with you but leave room for him to say he isn't.) What is the meaning of the throat-clearing, yawning, giggling, buzzing, quivering of voice, shouting?

What is the basis for this outburst? Is it a momentary upset, triggered either by the person's "feeling bad" or by some inadvertent or presumed slight? Or does he feel this strongly about the merits of the issue? (Should you "cool it," apologize, ignore him?)

Watch the body language: a shift forward or rearward in the chair; fidgeting; a wink; a nod; a clenching of a fist; a frown; a scowl; drumming of fingers on the desk. Was the body expression a reflex action, or was it intended? Was its purpose to express satisfaction, to relieve tension, to gain control of a conversation, meeting, organization, relationship?

Especially, read signals which indicate a desire by the other person to speak and to be heard. A slight opening of the mouth, accompanied by the intake of air, may say, "I've got something I'd like to mention." It's important that you learn to recognize and heed these listen-to-me-awhile signals, for if the other person has grown restless or inattentive, you aren't likely to regale him (inform him, persuade him) further. You might as well let him talk; then you can finish your story or try

Step Three: "Read"

to close out your deal.

Body language, which, no doubt, is as old as man himself, has within the last few years come into so much public discussion that it appears new. Body language always has been and always will be an important source of information, especially at the feeling level. Smart communicators recognize this and capitalize on it.

(For a deeper look into the art of reading body language, read Julius Fast's *Body Language*, M. Evans and Company, 1970.)

Perceptivity is one of the major components of creativity; indeed, to be perceptive is to be creative. You see, perceptivity involves more than the exercising of keen eyesight, acute hearing, etc. To be perceptive in the sense we're speaking of here requires that you bring something to the scene with you. A painter has more than a good eye, a deft hand, and a technical knowledge of how to mix colors. He brings something of himself — his experiences, his imagination, his life-view. He sees, interprets, relates, and uses harmony, contrast, direction, balance, rhythm, shade, tone. It's like this with the communicator. He brings something of himself to the conversation or group session. He sees, interprets, relates, and employs many elements — among them the elements I listed above as characterizing the painter.

There is a story of a great painter who was watching a sunset when his wife and daughter came out to summon him to the evening meal.

"Wait," he insisted. "I don't want to come in right now. I am studying the beauty in the skies."

The girl cocked her head from one angle to another. "That's nothing but a sunset," she said. "I can't see anything special, can you, mother?"

"Don't we wish we could?" the mother murmured. "Don't we wish we could!"

It's like that with the communicator. He sees things other people fail to see, ignore, or dismiss as unimportant.

Allow yourself to be impressed by the colors that surround you; permit yourself to be awed by the music of wind and water; let yourself be dazzled by starlight. God made a beautiful world and he intends for you to enjoy it. But let me emphasize that the most beautiful thing God created is people. Yes, read the nuances of nature, but do not neglect to read, also, the nuances of your own being and the nuances of your fellow men.

Elizabeth Barrett Browning, in her poem *Aurora Leigh*, gives us one of the best interpretations of what it means to be perceptive; or, as some people would say, to become skilled in the art of being percipient. She has this concept packed into a very few words:

> Earth s crammed with heaven,
> And every common bush afire with God;
> But only he who sees, takes off his shoes,
> The rest sit round it and pluck blackberries —

Perceptivity is highly individualized; each person operates within the range of his gifts. But perceptivity can be enhanced through training and experience. It's easy to set limits that are unrealistically confining.

Here are some of the benefits which derive from "reading":

1. *A new respect for the other person.* You learn to see him both as he is and as he can become. You respect him for what he is and for his potential. When he finds

that you accept and trust him, he will be encouraged to open himself up to you and to others, permitting him to grow. There can be no friendship of consequence without a feeling that with this person (this group), you can afford to bare your hopes, fears, and aspirations. You can quit playing games and begin wrestling with the real issues of life. But percipience can, of course, be employed for evil purposes as well as for good. (Witness that better than average reader of human nature, Adolf Hitler.)

2. *A new respect for the process, and the purposes, of communication.* As the creative possibilities open up to you, naturally you will find the process more exciting and more fulfilling. You will derive motivation to improve; still, you will develop a quality of patience, for you will discover that communicators are not born, nor are they developed overnight. You will also recognize, and accept, that pain accompanies major changes, and this understanding will give you holding power.

In Japan "watch parties" are held. Beginning with the rising of the moon, the party meets in a garden or park. There is an air of expectancy. No words are spoken as the flowers fold against the night cool. Mists creep in and silver the shrubs and grass. Small animals rustle, communicating with tiny sounds. The party lasts until the sun's rays lap up the gray sky. Each participant has given his complete attention to nature.

Have you enjoyed the companionship of someone who gave you the rapt attention which characterizes the watch party? Who evidenced the same high degree of expectation? There aren't many persons who have these traits, are there? And, looking back, I can see that the people who have read me well and have brought out the best in me have been a motley bunch, a strange mix of executive-types (most of them with sixteen to twenty years of formal education) and homespun philosopher types, many of whom didn't get beyond the tenth grade. Both types became experts in understanding, and relating to, people in general and individuals in particular. What did they have in common? Interest? Curiosity? Yes, but I would suggest that the main thing they possessed was *want to*.

Do you *want to*?

Step Three: "Read"

For Your Practice

1. I have suggested that one of the chief prerequisites for learning to read people is *want to*. Try an experiment in *wanting to*. Approach your next interpersonal encounter with a high degree of motivation and expectancy. During your meeting, recognize that in the present moment (from your existential position), this person is the most important person in the world. Afterward, reflect upon the experience. Did taking the other person(s) that seriously enrich the encounter and the relationship?

2. In the context of your experience from 1, above:
   (a) Recall instances when Jesus showed an extraordinary ability to read people.
   (b) Evaluate how this capacity and capability enhanced his ministry.

3. Answer these questions: Do you want to be accepted, but sometimes feel rejected? Do you wish to be esteemed, but sometimes feel inferior? Do you occasionally feel lonesome, but wish to be shared? Do you want to be understood, but are misunderstood? Do you want to be loved, but often feel neglected?

Now, look outward. From what you know about other people, would you say that many of them feel as you do?

4. During the next twenty-four hours, be alert for signals from people about you indicating that they are "hurting" after the fashion of the questions posed in 3, above. Remember, they aren't going to shout, "Hey, people, I feel lonely." Instead, they'll put out some

signs and feelers in the hope that someone will read them and ease their burden of uncomfortableness or desperation. During these twenty-four hours try to relate to people who feel rejected, inferior, lonesome, misunderstood, neglected.

5. During the next television show you watch, or the next movie or stage play you attend, pay special attention to nonverbal expressions the players employ. Group these expressions in categories — for example: "Facial Gestures," "Body Movements," etc.

6. Apply what you observed in 5, above, to a real-life situation in your place of business, home, or other meeting place. Note the nonverbal ways in which people about you reflect their feelings, but this time divide the expressions into two categories: "Intended or Contrived" and "Unintended or Subconscious."

7. Practice reading individuals in a variety of settings and circumstances. At a family meal when you tell a joke (well, *you* call it a joke), why does one person laugh while another "holds back"? In the church choir, why do some singers hold their music high and smile as they sing, while others don't? How did the minister come to have a particular mannerism? Why does a certain child in a group of children exaggerate? Why does a given person blush easily? How did this person become a back-slapper? Would you attribute the quietness of this individual to shyness, disinterest, inattention, inability to make up his mind, a reflective nature, discipline?

8. When you next come home in the evening, (or greet your spouse and/or children when they come home) — or when you arrive at your place of work — or when you

Step Three: "Read"

join a group at your club, church, etc.:
- (a) Read the group, individually and corporately.
- (b) On the basis of your reading, take steps to bring the group into closer harmony, a sense of belonging, a feeling of common purpose, etc. Afterward, evaluate the effectiveness of your input. Also, decide whether or not you had read the individuals and the group well.

9. How do you signal another person that you are ready to get your two cents' worth in? Had you ever really stopped to consider this question? During a twenty-four-hour period, "watch" yourself and see how you wedge yourself into agendas. At the same time, be alert for similar signals from other persons.

10. Television watchers come in all persuasions, some are hardly deserving of the tag "fan," while others are obvious fanatics. Take one or more persons whom you know to be light TV watchers. Try to read why they have so little enthusiasm for, or need of, television. Now try to read one or more persons who are inveterate TV watchers — how did they get to be this way? Are the pushes/pulls that make for TV watching obvious or subtle?

STEP 4 GAIN ATTENTION

We're neither generous enough nor impractical enough to be satisfied with merely preparing, listening, and "hearing." We also want to secure attention. People will give attention to that which promises to

- give pleasure and joy
- grant ego-satisfaction
- provide financial gain
- prevent embarrassment, financial loss, ill health, etc.

Don't *you* pay attention when a person or situation promises you a reward or threatens you?

"Hey, stop doing what *you're* doing and look at what *I'm* doing. Hear what *I'm* saying. I know you're looking my way, but pay closer attention. Give me your undivided attention. Tell me that I'm important, too."

We desire attention for any of innumerable reasons.

Step Four: Gain Attention

Getting attention is a way for us to preen our egos. Usually, we seek attention as the first step toward achieving a goal. But there are times when we want attention for someone else's benefit. Witness:

"John," cries Mary to her office-bound husband. "John —"

"I'm listening, I'm listening," John insists. "Mary, do you have my car keys?"

"You'll have to pick Janie up after school..."

"Baby," he shouts, "I'm in a hurry. Now, where are those keys? If I'm late again today..."

"If Janie's not right on time for her music lesson — well, we know what happens, don't we?"

"The keys!" John demands, rummaging his pockets and searching the kitchen.

"Here they are!" he shouts upon discovering the keys beside the telephone. "In this house, nothing is ever where it is supposed to be."

With that parting shot, John whisks out the door.

Did Janie miss her twelve-dollar music lesson? Did her teacher scold her? Did Mary scold John? Tune in tomorrow — *if* you can take any more.

Willing to try another?

"Harriet, will you please pay attention?" pleads the teacher.

Harriet is nine and in the fourth grade. She is far more interested in what she can see through the school window than what the teacher is saying. Harriet learned "all those old facts" a long time ago. Now she wants to learn something new.

"We're starting a new group project," the teacher explains. "This is something you'll all enjoy."

Harriet takes her chin out of her hands and turns back toward the teacher. She has an "I'll-give-her-another-chance" look on her bright little face.

"We're starting an ecology project. We're going to study streams and see if we can make them come alive again."

Harriet's eyes sparkle. She and the other students cheer. Here is something *important*! They can go to a nearby stream, note the presence or absence of living things, take samples of the water and check for contaminants, look at the contents through the microscope, and think of ways to undo man's insults to nature.

Gaining attention is essential to the person-to-person communication process. It is an art. It involves skills. How to gain attention can be learned! And the key is rather simple. Essentially, it's a matter of promising rewards or threatening punishment or deprivation.

Or look at it this way. You gain another person's attention when what you offer appeals to his native curiosity, taps a latent interest within him, or ties into an interest which is already manifest.

Let me describe the "Triple S Method" for gaining attention. It comprises three devices —

. a sharp sound or a slap
. the soft-and-still approach
. the simple skill of silence.

If you'll observe the work of the professionals, you'll see that they use the Triple S Method frequently.

An advertiser buying network time, with only thirty seconds or a minute available, wants to be sure he's gaining attention and holding it for that brief moment. In television commercials you'll find sharp sounds and

Step Four: Gain Attention

slaps: The producer zooms you into the middle of action; throws splashes of color at you; subjects you to the loud ticking of a clock, or the ticking of an acid stomach. He hits you with harsh ideas: "When a burglar strikes, you may lose property, but *you could lose a lot more!*"

The soft-and-still approach is ideally suited to selling some types of goods and services — for example, holiday homes. Rustling leaves, still water, a browsing deer, quiet companionship. The soft-and-still approach is more effective when used in combination with "a sharp sound or a slap" for contrast. Example: a frantic city scene, then a tranquil travel scene.

An example of the simple skill of silence is when the announcer asks a question, then inserts five seconds of silence. If anything will grab your attention on television, silence will.

You probably use the devices of the Triple S Method all the time. A mother raps on a door and calls sharply, "Johnny, open the door this minute!" Or a wife rubs her husband's back and asks, "Do you love me?" Or a boss looks an errant employee squarely in the eye — and remains silent for half a minute.

Pause for a moment and think of other applications for the Triple S Method.

Here are additional tips for gaining attention, gathered from a variety of sources:

Begin with the eyes. Make the person want to look at you or the object you are displaying. Cause him to gaze with curiosity, to scrutinize, to admire. Notice how you use your own eyes — they are the windows of your mind and soul.

If you are trying to gain a person's attention and he refuses to look directly at you, consider these two possibilities: (1) he doesn't consider you important, or (2) looking at you is painful (not because you're a monster, but for other reasons — for example, it may be that you're pressing him to accept a reality he doesn't want to face).

Test the importance of eye appeal. The next time you attend a lecture, sermon, or other speaking event, notice the way the speaker employs eye contact and eye movement. Also, you'll find that in a fairly intimate grouping, you can exercise considerable control over the speaker by giving him deliberate eye signals and other facial expressions. If you nod affirmatively, he'll likely plunge on with increased fervor. If you look at him incredulously, he'll likely back up and go over the material again.

Give the person reason to like you. If you've had previous contact with the person, then your past experiences will influence his response to you. If, on the other hand, this is a first acquaintance, you have only the present to work with (which is sometimes a blessing). Either way, you have to persuade him to accept you as someone who is interested in him and wants to serve his best interests.

People like to hear what they want you to say. They like to be complimented; they like to have their positions and attitudes reinforced. If you can honestly and constructively begin with a compliment or a reassuring remark, you're going to gain attention. At the same time, however, you must:

Be honest. Despite their hunger for good news, people

Step Four: Gain Attention 63

will not continue to give you their attention unless they find you to be truthful, motivated with integrity, and knowledgeable. Responsible persons will not accept a "snow job." In each situation, you have to delineate where "ego food" ends and "snowing" begins. Nearly anyone will respond positively to you if you treat him with dignity.

Approach attention-getting as a process. There are three stages: (1) you bring about a cessation of unrelated activity; (2) you bring the other person's eyes and other faculties to focus on you; (3) you set his 'computer' to programming the information you are giving, and (4) you work toward having the computer analyze the data and give Command Central a recommendation something like this: "Hey, this idea is important! Get with it!"

Take lessons from nature. John Portman of Atlanta, who has scored a number of architectural successes, studies elements in nature which captivate people — for example, cascading water, a cozy fire, trees and greenery, etc. He places units of these natural materials or phenomena (or simulations of them) along or near pathways. You, too, can capture attention by either incorporating natural elements into a setting or by vocalizing about nature.

You have, no doubt, noted that I admire salesmen and believe they have a lot to teach communicators who are engaged in other lines. Those who train salesmen use a device called A-I-D-A. (The letters are borrowed from the name of the opera "Aida.")

A-I-D-A means to get the
> Attention of the person you are trying to interest, and to

- *I*nterest the person by stimulating a
- *D*esire for the product, leading to the
- *A*ction necessary to complete the sale.

The principles of A-I-D-A, like the principles of the ACE Memory System, are simple. Again, do not let simplicity prejudice you.

You may ask, "What does salesmanship and A-I-D-A have to do with person-to-person communication in the sense we're talking about? Granted that not every person-to-person communication experience is for the purpose of selling, I would insist that the two activities have much in common. Often in person-to-person communication you are trying to "sell" information, an idea, a program, or yourself. In both sales and other interpersonal relationships, we speak of "transactions." The book *I'm OK, You're OK* is an interpretation of "transactional analysis."

"Red" Motley, one of the foremost experts on salesmanship, has said, "Selling is want creating." And so it is. Selling either (1) creates a new want, or (2) reaffirms or brings to the surface a want which has been repressed. The person-to-person communicator also creates wants. Where the salesman may convince me that I need a new house, the person-to-person communicator may persuade me that I want a new *me*. Hopefully, the salesman and the person-to-person communicator will go beyond merely exciting this want; hopefully, they will be sincere enough to want to help me fulfill my new (or intensified) desire. In the case of communication, the verbal exchange itself may satisfy my needs.

Our cries for attention begin at birth. The infant

Step Four: Gain Attention

wails, "Stop a minute and give me some attention, I'm hungry." Another cry says, "Hey, you left the safety pin unsnapped." And still another, "I'm lonely. I want some holding and rocking."

The struggle for attention continues throughout life — your life, my life, everyone's life. *Obtaining attention* is a primary step in communication. *Giving attention* is one of the most humanitarian things we can do. The more difficult task is *holding attention*. Unless the object or person before him is of extreme interest or importance to him, the average person will give his full attention for not more than five or ten seconds at the time. Will this short span of time be sufficient to serve your purpose — or can you extend this attention span? Herein lies success or failure.

As in all other phases of interpersonal communication, the attention-getting aspect is made challenging by individualized variances. The message isn't implicit in the method. Imagine a mother attempting to get the attention of her small child. She speaks to him several times to no avail, then gives him a sharp tap on the shoulder. Immediately, he looks up. Are we to conclude that a touch-tap means "Look up?" Does a touch-tap inherently convey a sense of frustration and impatience? No, the same kind of a tap can mean "Hey, I think you're great." The meaning is influenced by the situation.

Each person has to work out his own ways of gaining attention. You probably couldn't, on the spur of the moment, say what methods you employ. Ask a husband how he gets his wife's attention; then ask the wife how the husband gets her attention. Chances are, the answers will not be compatible.

Yes, our attention-getting mechanisms are individualistic. But there's a dark side. We also have our own individual ways of tuning people out. On occasion, this is a happy facility, but not usually.

What are the personal qualities that attract? A certain man or woman enters a room filled with people. Immediately, he/she gains attention — and holds it. Does the magnetism lie in physical attractiveness, grooming, dress, voice, presence, outgoing manner, charm? When it's impossible to say, we sometimes lump it all under "charisma."

Other people go ignored. Why? And then there are people whom we might call "promising" — who are pleasing at first, but begin to lose their appeal and even to grate on you after a while. A minister, teacher, parent, supervisor — these persons, because of their heavy exposure, are especially vulnerable to becoming abrasive. The distracting or offending feature may be a facial tic, a peculiar set of the jaw, a whining voice, an overused gesture, a slouch — these things start getting to you!

Remember, when I talk about gaining attention, I'm not speaking solely of a one-shot deal. Above all, I am trying to enhance your capacity for building *lasting* relationships. This suggests that you should inventory your 'tuning out' characteristics. Improve those that can be improved, accept those you can't do anything about. But even in the latter category — there is something you can do to offset them. You can enhance your "tuning in" qualities so that they will offset your handicaps. (There are beautiful people who have

Step Four: Gain Attention 67

hunched backs or pock-marked faces!) Prepare. Inform yourself. Listen. Show interest. Smile.

But first, you must *know* your situation. And even your best friends won't tell you — unless (1) they are exceptionally loyal friends, and (2) you can assure them that you really do want to know.

Develop at least one friendship which permits you to express your personal concerns. The key words here are mutuality and trust.

If you do not have a friend like this, why not talk with your minister? Discuss your "failures" with him. He'll listen. But remember that he may have a demanding schedule — make an appointment! Also, don't expect very much specific advice; instead expect a friendly ear.

If you think you've got the other person's attention, how can you be sure? Or, how can you know whether you are *continuing* to hold his attention, once you've gained it?

Here are some techniques:

Ask a question. "I obtained this data from the lab. Is that the best source?"

Pose a problem. "Julie, your coming in late is creating family conflict. What can we do about it?"

Ask for an interpretation. "It seems to me that this project is finished. How do you see it?"

Be silent. Wait for the other person to respond. Two to one (assuming he's awake) — he'll fill the silence that you've created with some sort of expression. If he doesn't, you can be rather sure he isn't riding your train of thought.

If you wish to be more direct, say (for example): "I'm concerned about this schism in our group." Stop right there. Wait for an answer. If no response is given, you know that *your* concern hasn't become *his* concern.

Use a mechanical device. Shift forward in your chair. Tap on the table. Ask if the other person wishes to stop for refreshment. Mechanical methods *do* get attention: The telephone rings, asking, "Is there anyone at home? If so, someone here wants to talk to you." You pick it up.

Ring a "bell." It usually works. Sometimes you don't have to resort to a technique to learn that somebody wasn't attentive — it's all too obvious:

"The Browns are coming to dinner tonight, you know."

"No, I didn't know. Why didn't you tell me?"

"I did tell you."

"My, I must not have been listening."

And these were two highly educated people, mind you. I wonder if the one had "educated" himself not to listen to the other. The Busy B's — barriers, blocks, and bars — do their dirty work among all persons, regardless of education or social status.

Gain attention. Trying to gain attention is an honorable pursuit — *if* — *if* you have a good reason for gaining attention. Some good reasons: Because you're hurting physically, mentally, morally, or spiritually. Because you have love to share. Because you have a willing and interested ear to lend. Because you have a valid product or service to sell, or a valid idea to convey. Or you may wish to persuade another person to do something for someone else.

But you gain nothing if you gain nothing but attention. If you cry, "Wolf!" you gain attention, yes. But

Step Four: Gain Attention

the townspeople will not think kindly of you if you follow with "ha, ha!" A woman may gain attention with false eyelashes, but (unless she has a winsome facility for bailing herself out), she isn't going to get the kind of attention she intended if an eyelash falls off.

"My son and I don't communicate any more. I can't even get his attention."

Think about it a moment, Mom or Dad. Think, Son, Daughter, Member, Citizen, Friend. *What is it* that you wish to communicate?

Talk, talk, talk. The world is full of talk. What the world needs now is *love, love, love.*

Gain attention? Yes. But take the other person's interest in you seriously. Don't disappoint him; don't let him down.

For Your Practice

1. List some mechanical attention-grabbers. Begin with bells. List settings where bells are used to gain attention. Now list some visual attention-grabbers. Of these, which tend to *prevent* physical harm? Which may *cause or contribute* to physical harm?

2. Keep your notebook or a piece of paper handy in your home or place of work. Over a period of several hours, note instances of attention-grabbing. Was the appeal justified? Was it appropriately made?

3. "Listen" to yourself and catch the methods you employ to gain attention. Afterward, consider whether or not you were aware of the range of devices you employ.

4. A "beautiful" woman can launch a thousand ships or stop a thousand eyes on the street. An attractive man can sell a thousand contracts or win a thousand friends. Think of the most winsome people you've ever met. What are (were) their winning qualities? Would it be possible for you to develop one or more of these qualities in your own person and life?

5. During a sermon, lecture, or other formal speech, note the speaker's "tricks of the trade" for gaining and holding attention. (Note 6, below)

6. On the occasion of 5, above, note mannerisms and other quirks that annoy, distract, or otherwise mar the speaker's presentation. Reflect upon your own idiosyncrasies. Do you suppose that people are reacting to them in the same way you reacted to the speaker's (above)?

Step Four: Gain Attention 71

7. The next time you crave attention from a family member, co-worker, or close friend, and you aren't getting it, try the direct approach. Just say, "Hey, I need you to listen to me a minute." Afterward, consider the result. Should you use the direct method more often? What are the advantages and disadvantages of the direct method?

8. Recall one or more events where you tried to gain someone's attention and failed. What were the consequences? Reflect on each case individually: Do you wish you had succeeded in gaining attention? Are you glad you didn't?

9. After you secure the attention you seek, what planned actions will you take to justify his gift of his time, interest, and energy?

10. Can you remember any methods God used — as related in the Bible — to secure the attention of those who were supposed to obey and serve Him?

STEP 5 DECLARE

You've prepared. You've listened. You've "read." You've rung your bell and attracted attention. Now, *declare*! To declare is to

- state your goal
- reveal your convictions
- make your pitch
- get it off your chest
- persuade.

Declaring is the heart, bone, and muscle of the communication process. If you do not declare well, all of your efforts to prepare, listen, "read," and gain attention will come to naught.

Declaring is an art. It involves skills. Here are some of the basic requirements for effective declarations:

Step Five: Declare

- You must have a clearly defined goal.
- You must have something to say.
- You must know how to say it.
- You must know when to quit, and how.
- You must sustain mutual respect.

Again, these ideas are so simple! But before you brand me a simpleton for even mentioning them, let me share with you an observation made across more than half a century. The best lecturers on communication speak in the *simplest* terms. The more expert the authority, the less complicated the approach.

We've been communicating all our lives, which means that we know *something* about the process. But: (1) we don't know it all; (2) what we've learned, we may not have assimilated logically; and (3) we don't practice what we *do* know.

A salesman must know how to declare or he becomes a mere ordertaker. In special training sessions, salesmen are taught to write out, memorize, and rehearse their presentations, and to prepare against interruptions and exceptions. All of this is done for just one person — the *next* customer.

"Prepare" must come before "Declare."

Salesman Tom Brown learned this truth the hard way. Tom was trying to sell heavy-duty bolts to officials representing the engineering and purchasing departments of a giant automobile assembly plant. He had convincingly demonstrated the quality of his company's bolts, and the officials had indicated that the price was reasonable.

Tom closed his sales pitch with enthusiasm. He didn't

know precisely how many bolts the assembly plant would buy, but certainly this would be the biggest order that his small company had ever received.

The prospective purchasers were enthusiastic, too.

"Very impressive, Mr. Brown," a spokesman said. "Now, if your rate of delivery will meet our schedules, we can do business. Of course, we will be looking to you to supply our total needs since we want the maximum discount for quantity."

When Tom heard the quantity, he was dumbfounded. He had failed to mention his plant's maximum production capacity in his sales talk, leaving the buyers to think that quantity was no problem. The specified need would exceed the total output of Tom's plant, which was operating two shifts.

Tom tried to hide his surprise and reassure the officials that his company would be able to meet their need. His company would initiate a third shift, he said.

The officials saw that Tom was flustered, and his being unnerved caused them to lose confidence. They knew that only under the most ideal circumstances can a third shift operate without a considerable elevation in costs and a deterioration of quality.

The officials politely said "no," and when Tom persisted, they rather curtly said "good day."

On the drive home, Tom recognized that he had put *declare* ahead of *prepare*. If he had learned of the quantity in advance, he could have included in his presentation some ideas for holding down costs and preserving quality on a third shift. Now, as he thought about it, there were some very interesting possibilities...

"Oh, well."

Step Five: Declare 75

When you declare, you place what you wish to communicate in a beautiful wrapping, tie a ribbon around it, and then present the package to the recipient. There's an excellent kit for packaging your product called "The Package Of P's."

The P's are:

Purpose. You must have a clearly defined purpose, clearly defined objectives, clearly defined goals.

Preparation. You dignify what you are doing with honest preparation.

Plan of action. You prepare for the expected and the unexpected.

Presentation. You make your presentation in a clear, concise, honest, and interesting manner.

Poise. A skilled communicator has poise! Poise is the ribbon that ties the package. Sometimes even the best communicator will get thrown off balance, and he may let his emotions get the upper hand; however, he will persist in attempting to recover his poise.

There are some notorious "poise-wreckers." One wrecker is having someone vent his anger at you. Only if you strive diligently to keep your cool will you be able to remain on the track. If you are derailed, get back on and running right away. A hasty *word*, like a hasty shot, can be devastating. You won't always be able to maintain your poise (I know!), but you can learn from your mistakes. You can improve.

Persuasion. "You can catch more flies with honey than with vinegar."

There is no single secret to persuading; you will spend the rest of your life learning to persuade. But this is one of the most appealing and challenging P's in the communication package. Why? Because persuasion is a gentle word. A successful presentation is packed with persuasion — gentle, kind, and courteous. At times, persuasion takes the form of humor, sometimes praise, sometimes a gentle rebuke, sometimes inspiration, at other times sympathy.

If you refuse to admit that *he may be right* and *you may be wrong*, you will never become persuasive. No "Big I, little u" here.

Give the other person good reasons for changing his mind or his way of life. Study his needs. Read his words and his body language. Study his eyes, facial expressions. If you read "rejection," change your course.

Passion. Without passion, declaration is lifeless. This final "P" in your package involves two sets of emotion — your own and the other person's. The cold-hearted, shrewd, and indrawn person never achieves real success in person-to-person communication.

Here, then, is your "Package of P's": Purpose — Preparation — Plan of action — Presentation — Poise — Persuasion — Passion.

Have you accepted and planted the "Package of P's"? If you have, you're ready for the "Envelope of E's":

Excitement. Not only must you believe in your idea or cause and its benefits (passion), but you must also fire this other person with the zeal which activated you. Each presentation must be shared in the attitude of newness.

Energy. This second "E" is constant, creative expectancy. All leaders are charged with mental and physical energy. They may also have charisma, which is a projection of power and value. You sense the power

Step Five: Declare

you've been given. You feel the purpose. You are conscious of controlled dynamic energy. You have confidence in this commitment. You are ready to face disappointment and discouragement, but you move forward with the knowledge that, ultimately, success is ahead.

Enthusiasm. "Enthusiasm makes the difference." Dr. Norman Vincent Peale made this phrase immortal in the title of a best seller intended for salesmen, lecturers, and other persons who wish to learn the art of communication. Even if you are a person of mediocre talent, average ideas, and a record of meager accomplishments, you can nonetheless develop the art of enthusiasm.

Excitement — plus energy — plus enthusiasm. These dynamic qualities will multiply your chances for success in any communication effort. How do you acquire this zip code to success?

I've found that the basic determinant is whether you regard your task as worthwhile. You have just *so much* time and energy. Screen the channels into which you may direct this time and energy. That is, be sure that your cause is worth the effort. Then, learn all you can about the subject and the persons involved. The more you learn, the more enthusiastic you'll become. If you don't become enthusiastic, ask, "Is this task really worth it?" You may decide to drop your goal right there.

If you "hire out" to make your living, I'll grant that you don't always have an opportunity to select projects — certainly, you won't have a chance to be overly "picky." But remember, the self-employed person isn't exactly a "free agent," either. And a good boss isn't going to relish keeping a competent and dedicated worker on a project he detests. Use the P's and E's to gain the task you would relish handling.

Once I've decided that *this* is what I want to do, and *here* is where I want to invest my time and energy — and once I've learned I can succeed and have developed my skills — when these conditions have been met, I somehow find the energy I need. It's just there (in my bones?), ready to be drawn upon.

When my cause is right, God sees that I have the energy I require to put the project over. I depend on this energy source, and I recommend it to you.

So — choose carefully, prepare well, and conserve your time and energy for matters that count.

A qualifying note: I do not mean to suggest that every communication effort is a rousing one. There are times when condolence and silent appreciation are to be projected. But always communicate with earnestness and sincerity, and your message will get through. If you don't know what to say, say nothing — just *be* there, letting your presence express your concern.

I've given you some P's and E's. I would also like to recommend to you a couple of S's. These S's are Signs and Symbols.

Signs and symbols have always held a high place in men's lives and in history. God put a bright star in the heavens as a sign that Jesus Christ the Savior had been born. The Bible is replete with signs and symbols: A cradle, wise men, precious gifts, the flood, a dove, fire, water, good grain and tares, lilies of the field, birds of the air. Signs and symbols are loaded with meaning; they are freighted with messages.

Step Five: Declare

Signs and symbols can express love and loyalty — for example, a band of gold around the third finger of the left hand, or the emblem of a fraternal order worn in the lapel. They can express expectancy — a bouquet of flowers, a new hairdo. Or — a stork!

Signs and symbols, when appropriately used, can set the stage for your declaration, or strengthen it otherwise. Signs and symbols may be tied to the tradition of the group (or to personal friendship), to the season, or to the theme of your presentation. Perhaps I'm being rather loose with my definition of signs and symbols, but I would include a warm handshake, calling for the other person in your car, having table decorations, remembering his birthday, refreshing the other person's memory of past ties.

Become familiar with the use of signs and symbols generally. Beyond this, learn to "read" the other person's own signs and symbols, as well as how he responds to yours. A particular sign or symbol, when used in a particular way, can be detrimental or evil — for example, a sign used to place a hex on another person. A sign or symbol can be poor psychology, as, for example, opening a meeting aimed at reconciliation with a group of dissenting militants by having a flag ceremony.

Be sensitive to the other person's personality. A pat on the shoulder may thaw a cold type of individual — on the other hand, it might make his blood boil. He might consider it "forward" of you. Much depends on the general tone of the relationship and the prevailing circumstances. Your pat on the shoulder could spring naturally from your desire to show warmth of feeling, or it could be contrived — and show it!

Both before and during your declaration, read your audience. To build a "pat" speech, no matter how good it is, isn't enough. If you don't remain alert for crosscurrents, you won't be able to apply the rudder and stay on course.

Assume that you are at a City Council meeting for the purpose of persuading the city fathers to build a youth center. As the councilmen deal with other matters, you use your waiting time to good advantage. You watch the councilmen and listen to them, picking up clues as to their mind set.

"Our crime rate is up five per cent from last month. We need more policemen, and at better salaries . . . stronger gun laws . . . curfews . . ."

You are listening to a very "conservative" man. You observe the other councilmen. They are responding affirmatively with words and body language. The speaker seems to have eight out of ten of the group with him.

You decide to junk most of your speech. Instead, you will promote a youth center chiefly in terms of a more responsible, more peaceful city:

"A youth center will reduce mischief-type activities, which currently absorb much of our officers' time. They will be able to spend their time combatting crime. A center will provide wholesome activities . . . respect for the community . . . creative involvement in the group process . . ."

As you speak, you read the group. Affirmative nods tell you that you were wise to approach the council "where they are."

Declarations of excellence have an enduring quality;

Step Five: Declare 81

some of them have become idioms of history. Consider:

Shakespeare's "Julius Caesar": "Friends, Romans, countrymen, lend me your ears; I come to bury Caesar, not to praise him."

Patrick Henry: "I know not what course others may take; but as for me, give me liberty, or give me death!"

Abraham Lincoln: ". . . It is for us, the living, rather to be dedicated here to the unfinished work they have thus far so nobly advanced . . ."

Ruth: "Where you go, I will go, and where you stay, I will stay. Your people shall be my people, and your God my God." (Ruth 1:16 NEB).

Of course, some classics lose their luster — if, indeed, they ever had much luster. Times and attitudes change.

Some losers:

"This is going to hurt me more than it will you."

"Remember, I'm doing this for your own good."

In making a declaration, you have to take into consideration the audience, the time, and other factors. And don't always take it for granted that what you propose is for the other person's own good, or is necessarily right. Let the other person(s) participate in that judgment. A mother told me that she stopped the practice of physically punishing her son when, on one occasion, he *declared* himself by looking her squarely in the eye without flinching. This mother was forced to ask herself: "Am I punishing the child for a wrong, or am I venting my anger on him because he is convenient?"

Children learn, sooner than parents think, to perceive a situation and to declare.

Let's examine another communication episode involving a child:

Bill was reading a "how-to" article on camping in the deep woods when a stone shattered his living room window. He leaped from his chair and charged out the door. He had told his ten-year-old son to stop playing with that slingshot! Bill bore down on the startled youngster, concurrently bewailing the cost of replacing the window.

"This is for your own good," Bill shouted as he grabbed his son's arm. "I'm going to spank you hard and throw that slingshot away!"

Bill was venting so much anger that any corrective value is doubtful.

Bill had been wrapped up in planning for a family camping trip, and he had failed to let the boy participate in the planning. He had himself bought the slingshot for his son, but he had neglected to instruct the son or caution him concerning its use.

Bill could have instructed the son to stay in the *back* yard. Better, he could have diverted his son's interest into some other activity. Best, he could have pointed out to the lad that a crowded neighborhood is no place to practice with a slingshot, but that in camp there would be nice, round pebbles, and near camp there would be good places to shoot them.

Bill had not taken the time either to *prepare* or to *declare*.

You have reached the time for declaration. Utilize your full resources as you declare:
. Speak up now
. Speak out now

Step Five: Declare

- Communicate now
- If necessary, try again

Say to yourself: "The time is *now*, the place is *here*. I will never have this same opportunity again, and if I muff it, I may never have another opportunity like it."

Generally speaking, your investment of time and energy in your preparation and your declaration must be governed by the value you place on the subject and the situation. Still, be mindful that:

1. You never know what a casual conversation may mean in terms of an idea developed, a friendship formed, a life enriched.

2. Your presence and interest may be just what the other person needs. For him, the present minute may be critical.

You cannot foretell what rewards may germinate from an inauspicious introduction or meeting. Often I have done a slight favor for someone to find him, at a later time, doing a great favor for me.

Although expectation of personal reward is not the best motivation for interpersonal relationships, rewards do ensue. You show an interest in a person of little or no influence today; tomorrow he's your boss. Some say that success depends upon being at the right place at the right time. But, there's a line in the sweepstakes advertisements, "You do not have to be present to win." You *don't* have to be there in order to win — not if there is someone present who will speak up and speak out in your behalf.

For Your Practice

1. Try an experiment in human relations. Select someone to whom you've been meaning to give a pat on the back. Give that pat now. (Or, if you've heard someone else say something complimentary about this person, relay the compliment now. It doesn't matter if the compliment doesn't seem very significant; merely relate it with genuine enthusiasm and appreciation.)

Note the immediate response. Later, evaluate what the compliment has done in the way of long-range friendship, conversation, trust. Are you glad you declared your appreciation without delay?

2. Prepare now to declare at your next meeting, interview, or appointment, etc. (It may be an appointment with a teacher, a conference with your supervisor.)

Who will be there? What mood can you expect?

What is your role?

What should you bring with you in terms of a statement, a plan for action, or knowledge, skills, or materials?

What compliments or other reassuring elements can you share?

How can you point out failures or shortcomings in a friendly, constructive way (*if* such observations are warranted)?

Would an aggressive or a passive role be appropriate? Will you be able to control your emotions? Or, on the other hand, do you lack interest?

After the event, reflect whether or not your preplanning helped, and how.

Step Five: Declare

3. Study declarations by professionals in a newspaper or magazine, on television or the radio, from the pulpit — or from a panhandler on the street. Analyze the declaration:
    (a) Had your attention been seized?
    (b) Did the declarer make you feel good? Inferior?
    (c) Did the declarer seem sincere? Did he win your confidence?
    (d) Was the declaration interesting, concise, clear?
    (e) Was it effective?
    (f) What changes would you have made?

4. If there ever was a time when the world moved at a leisurely pace, that time isn't now. Today, time is money. The world will not give you a moment's notice unless there's a good reason. Brevity is essential.

Do you take seriously your use of other people's time? When you call a meeting, do you stop to think how much the employment of this group of people would cost you if you had to pay them?

The following exercise has two purposes. First, it will give you a feeling as to whether others are economical with your time; second, it will let you practice conciseness of expression.

Take an editorial from a newspaper or magazine. An editor has asked you to reduce its length by half. (You can either paste the editorial on a larger sheet of paper and work in the margins, or you can rewrite it.) Now, at the editor's request, reduce the editorial to a single paragraph for radio broadcast. Finally, prepare for Page One a one-sentence blurb which captures the intent of the editorial.

5. There are persons who are notoriously bad at

declaring. Bring to mind several such persons. What are their failings? How, do you suppose, did they get this way? Can you help them without doing lasting injury? Can you *declare* to a person about his own inability to declare?

6. The following paragraphs represent a speech made by the chairman of a conservation group fighting the pollution of a creek and harbor. As you read the speech, be alert for P's, E's, S's, and other devices; also, judge whether the reaction may be what the speaker intended to provoke.

"Neighbors, we live in a beautiful little town. We've invested our lives in this place, as did our families before us. We are proud of our community and we want to preserve and protect it.

"Now, no community wants to be unfair to, or to hurt, an industry that contributes to its economy. From the standpoint of payrolls and from the standpoint of supporting civic endeavors, Goop Chemical has been a good neighbor. But as fond as we may be of the people who run Goop, we cannot afford to let them ruin Sandy Creek and Big Harbor.

"You have in your hands excerpts from a report made by the State Department of Conservation at our request. The full report is on file at City Hall. This report shows why you commercial fishermen can't make ends meet, and why you sports fishermen aren't having any luck. And why those of you who, like me, bought summer places on the beach cannot use that beach. The report also says that things will get worse if they do not get better.

"There is an answer to our problem, a settling

Step-Five: Declare

basin, which would require of Goop an outlay of only $700,000. This is a small amount, a fraction of their profits. Tonight, we want you to sign a petition that will impress upon Goop's leaders our desire for them to build that settling basin. I ask you, is $700,000 too high a price to pay for restoring our God-given beaches to the state that he intended, or for assuring health to our families? I urge you, sign the petition."

7. List three items you liked about this declaration and list three statements that offended you.

8. Were you moved enough to walk forward and sign the petition?

9. What plans are you going to make *tonight* for tomorrow's opportunities "to declare"?

STEP 6 INTERPRET

To interpret is to
- . Integrate and evaluate feedback
- . Assess changes in the situation
- . See what help is needed
- . Decide to drive on — or quit.

A good driver sees the "big picture." So does a good manager. Consciously and subconsciously, he is alert to hundreds of bits of information concerning conditions and events as they roll out before him. Each bit of data is interpreted, then dismissed, heeded, or stored for later evaluation. This process is *interpretation*.

The President examines the country's present situation from the perspective of the near and distant past and the near and distant future. His "State of the Union" message is interpretation.

Step Six: Interpret

Each of us, from time to time, has need of interpretation. We need to see how well the pieces of a particular project are fitting together. Beyond this, we need to stand back and view the "big picture" of our lives. We need to deliver (mainly to ourselves) our personal "State of Me" message.

Over periods of weeks and months, we initiate, or submit to, hundreds and thousands of forces of change — *and we change!* We're not the same persons that we were an hour ago, a day ago, a month ago. It's imperative that we recognize the changes, interpret them, and use our understanding of them to shape our destiny.

One of the problems of interpreting (and especially of interpreting our personal situations) is the difficulty of "getting a handle" on the problem. What question is the right question to ask?

I was having lunch at the Tower Club with Mr. Wright, who is a business consultant. The dining room afforded a view of the city and blue-hazed mountains beyond. Our conversation drifted to the desire of the younger generation to know, "Who am I?"

"There is," Mr. Wright said, "a more important question that the young people might ask — one that businessmen are continually asking."

"More important than 'Who am I?' Then what is it?"

Looking out upon the magnificent view, he replied: "Instead of 'Who am I?' they should be asking, 'How am I doing?' "

"Who am I?" is a worthy question. But, as Mr. Wright emphasized, we must also ask ourselves, "How am I doing?"

How am I doing? Well, I'm doing *different* things than before; I'm also doing old things in new ways, and with varying degrees of effectiveness. Change makes life both interesting and challenging. To shape and control (even cope with) change requires communication, and interpretation is a vital step in the process.

Consider our journey together. "How are we doing?" We started in the foothills of Prepare and Listen. We scaled the heights of Attention, "Read," and Declare. Now, during a breathing spell, we are perched on a precarious ledge called Interpret before tackling the pinnacle, Ask for Action.

"Interpret" may sound confusingly like "Read," which was Step Three. They are essentially the same except for scope. To "read" is to use all of your faculties to ascertain the real meaning of what a person or group is doing or saying *at a given moment*. To "interpret" is to consolidate your sequence of readings and, on the basis of them and other data, to evaluate your total situation. This includes your prospect for success or the threat of failure. To "read" is to look at the *little* picture; to "interpret" is to view the *big* picture.

"Read" is *where you are*, while "interpret" is between *where you are* and *where you're going*. "Interpret" is a way to get there.

Nowadays, individuals and groups are so busy "minding the store" that they have little time or disposition for engaging in interpretation. But the wise individual, and the wise leader, recognizes that to take time for evaluation is really to save time.

Step Six: Interpret

You have "read" the individual or the group, both before and after making your declaration. Now you interpret. You evaluate the state of the relationship, the direction and momentum of the action. You do this in the broad context of who you are, who the other person is, and how you're doing.

When you're in doubt as to whether you are proceeding toward your goal, employ additional interpretation. Then you'll know how to respond.

If there is confusion over the facts or the issue, say, "I probably didn't make that clear. Let's have another look. If anyone has a question, please interrupt me and ask it."

Once you have taken a second run, test to see if the replay really has clarified things. Invite questions or comments on *specifics*. Or say, "I'm glad we're so alert. Shall we move on and look at the proposal in greater detail, or do you have further questions?"

If, as you near conclusion, you are unsure whether there is concensus, or whether all important points are understood, take this approach: "Before we take formal action, we want to be sure we've made everything clear and that everyone has had a chance to make his contribution. Do we have further questions or comments?"

If the group has been working hard and long, you may ask if they'd like to take a break. Do not, however, forfeit momentum if a critical decision is about to be made.

After action has been taken, you may want to compliment the group on its attentiveness, cooperation, etc. If you sense negative feelings (maybe someone is nursing a personal hurt), you can (in a positive, yet sensitive, way) deal with these feelings.

Some persons are afraid of interpretation. They fear that someone will ask an embarrassing question, be critical of someone else in the group, or suggest that the current effort may fail.

But look at it this way: There is *going to be* interpretation, whether it takes place here and now, on the one hand, or away from here and later, on the other. So, why not get everything out on the table now, while the matter is fresh in everyone's mind? This way, everyone has a chance to participate in the evaluation. To wait may invite distortions and recriminations.

The good leader will point out that interpretation isn't intended to prove someone right and someone else wrong. The purpose is to be sure that everyone's together — either that, or to ensure that everyone is thoroughly acquainted with the basis of whatever differences exist. The same purpose applies to interpretation as between two persons, too.

Again, I think we can learn something from salesmen, who are excellent communicators.

A salesman wanted to introduce a new product to the president of a large organization. The president was known to be contemptuous of salesmen. The only way the salesman could get an audience was to promise to make his presentation short and snappy.

"Mr. Smith, I'd like to show you a new product..."

"Listen here, young man, I don't have time to look at all the crazy things that you people are bringing on the market these days."

The salesman recognized that he had led off with a trite introduction. He recognized also that he was about

Step Six: Interpret

to get the gate. He remembered that someone had told him Mr. Smith couldn't resist an opportunity to give his opinion on anything that came down the pike. So he said:

"Mr. Smith, I acknowledge that my chief reason for coming here is to sell you this product. But I'm also terribly interested in your ideas concerning the product's design, from the viewpoint of an experienced manufacturer. We believe we have a good product here and we want to be sure it's presented attractively."

The company president took the product, examined it, and made a few suggestions for improving the design. He additionally made a few gratuitous suggestions concerning the product generally. And, he ordered a large shipment for his own company.

The president sold himself after he had been invited to participate. True, if there had been no real need for the product, there likely would have been no sale. But a need didn't guarantee a sale, either.

Often, we cannot be sure of our estimates as to whether or not an idea, product, or service will appeal to the other person; but if we invite him to participate in an evaluation, he will come to his own decision, which may or may not be favorable to us. If he *does* buy, he won't have a sour taste in his mouth from "oversell."

If, in advance of the "moment of truth" (when you will call for action), you obtain a person's participation, you unobtrusively move him toward ratification or acquiescence. If he objects, you will have the opportunity to resolve your differences. If you cannot win him over, you will at least have the advantage of knowing how he stands.

Say that a chief executive has a plan which he'd like his board of directors to approve, but he senses that it wouldn't fare well if offered cold in a board meeting. In advance of the meeting, he calls on each member, outlines his plan, and invites questions and suggestions. If he is unable to convince a sufficient number of board members of the merits of his plan, he will drop it or defer it. But if a majority of directors either embrace the plan or decline to object to it, then the executive can be relatively sure of a favorable vote when the board meets. Persons who have a strong sense of integrity will rarely reverse an earlier commitment or even a tacit approval.

This same approach can be taken in almost any organization. But keep in mind these flags of caution:

- If you ask for criticism and get it, you'd better demonstrate that you have considered it carefully, else you may alienate the person who gave it.
- You must be careful not to create a game of power politics, where one member is played against another.
- You must avoid any hint of "railroading." You don't want to give the impression that you had to "clear it" with Mr. Big to keep him from being offended.
- Don't count your chickens prematurely; group dynamics may alter individual stances and throw you for a loss.

Interpretation can clarify, create understanding, and promote unity — or keep disagreement open and honest. But interpretation, when it is either sloppily handled or

Step Six: Interpret

interposed at the wrong moment, can be devastating. As I said earlier, many persons fear the exposure that interpretation entails.

At a PTA meeting, the chairman of the budget committee presented his proposal and moved for its adoption. There was a perfunctory second. Routinely, the president said, "Is there any discussion?" A member rose and proceeded to lay out several good, penetrating questions. The chairman was taken by surprise. He had expected a routine response. Not within his memory had anyone asked any questions. He showed resentment, and the meeting was thrown into an uproar.

Don't be afraid to invite interpretation; indeed, encourage it! But first, do your homework to be sure you can handle the device effectively.

If you're afraid you'll lose your composure, work hard at developing poise. Determine that on *this* occasion, at least, you're going to remain cool. If you lack technical information, either obtain this data or have someone on hand who can supply it. Anticipate questions and prepare to handle them.

Here are some additional tips on how to use interpretation to strengthen your position:

1. Invite suggestions. If you have employed the P's and E's, you can afford to do this.

2. Summarize formal presentations and informal discussion.

3. Be sure that you have been understood. (Caution! Don't ask this question bluntly.)

4. Clarify any cloudy issues.

5. Discover whether your ideas are being accepted. In a subtle way, ask for feedback.

6. If the feedback stings, count to ten; meanwhile, smile! Poise is the big thing here. Try to separate elements of *personal* criticism, as contrasted with criticism of your ideas. If the criticism is patently personal or has personal overtones, *this* may not be the time to deal with it.

7. Introduce criticism with an affirmative remark: "Ben, I like your idea about getting these important people here — they certainly would gain considerable exposure in the press for us. Still, I just wonder whether the publicity would justify the expense, our financial situation being what it is. What do you think? (Contrast this with, "Ben, I just don't think we can do that.")

8. Offer options and feel the group out concerning the options.

9. Develop a consensus; if required or desirable, take a vote.

In this chapter, we've given most of our attention to the use of interpretation in group process. Interpretation is also an important aid in one-to-one communication.

By reading the other person and interpreting his life-situation and his mood, you sense whether he is wanting to tell, or listen; give, or receive — or engage in a balanced exchange.

Whatever his situation, your first step is to affirm him as a person and as a friend. If he has the glow of a recent achievement or the anguish of a serious reversal to share with you, he wants to know that you're giving him your full attention and that you are interested. So, acknowledge him: "It's good to be with you again. Tell me about yourself."

If the other person is distraught or is trying to resolve

Step Six: Interpret

a crisis in his life, again his most urgent need is for you to affirm the reality and importance of his situation. "You're really hurting, aren't you? I'm truly sorry."

Identifying with a distressed person can be very helpful to him: "I know what you're going through. Someone close to me was killed in an automobile accident." Or, "I often have these feelings of worthlessness, myself."

Your friend may need a friendly ear more than he needs explicit advice. In any event, *listen*! If, however, you persist in maintaining absolute silence, he may mistake your quietness for disinterest — either this, or he may become self-conscious over talking so much. You can reassure him by nodding appreciatively or making affirmatory comments: "Yes, I see."

You may also employ a device which professional counselors use a great deal (more than the persons with whom they counsel would recognize). This is the *reflective* expression, either a question or a statement. As does the simple affirmation, the reflective expression says, "I'm here, I'm interested, and I'm following your conversation." It additionally says, "Please go on." And it may give a nudge of direction: "Yes, would you please tell me how he reacted?" Or, "here's the part I'd like to hear next . . ."

A reflective expression, as the name suggests, doesn't impart very much, if any, information. At times, it is essentially a repetition of something the other person said: "You were embarrassed, you say?"

Other reflective expressions:
"What did you do then?"
"I can see that you were angry."

"Do you think you'll get over this soon?"

"Well, at least that's the way you heard it, huh?"

By using reflective expressions, you get the picture laid out before you. More importantly, the other person lays the picture out before himself. *You* have served to keep him plugging away; you may also have kept him honest with himself. What you have done is to "walk with him" through his problem or disappointment.

Once the situation has been described, you can decide whether you should offer direction or not. You may decide that it wouldn't be helpful for you to suggest a solution. In this case, you may suggest a process: "What you have to do, I think, is to . . . and then . . ." Or you may choose only to express regret over whatever has happened and say that the other person can be sure you'll be thinking about him or that you'll remember him in your prayers.

Your friend may, however, already be wallowing in self-pity and need very little additional sympathy. Moreover, he may be blind to the fact that he himself contributed to the situation which now distresses him. He may be filled with unreasonable and self-destructive resentment of other persons. In these circumstances, he may need to be reminded that *he* is the one who's going to have to work through his situation — that only he can bring it to an ultimate resolution. He may additionally need to be reminded of his own responsibilities. Sometimes this point can be made by saying, "(Name) is counting on you, and I, too, know that you can do it."

Here is where mutuality pays off. You must have earned *access through demonstrated interest* if you are to speak frankly (if discreetly) with a person concerning

Step Six: Interpret 99

personal problems. If your relationship has the dimensions of enduring value, the conversation may go like this:

"Those joggers say they're going to kill my dog."

"I'm sorry to hear that. I know it disturbs you greatly."

"Why don't they do their running on another street. There are plenty more."

"Yes, but I don't guess you can realistically expect them to avoid your street, since the streets are public. Too, there's a law requiring that dogs be leashed."

"I know, but my family just won't take precautions to keep the dog inside the house. They let him out."

"It would seem to me that in view of the current threat, they would take this responsibility more seriously."

"That dog wouldn't hurt anyone. She's just being playful."

"She is a friendly dog, all right. But, you know, I guess there is something about German shepherds that frightens some people — for one thing, they're so powerful."

"Imagine, those people say they're going to kill my dog!"

"That's terrible. Why do people like that, who are so insistent upon their own rights under the law, shut their eyes to their own obligations? Certainly, to kill your dog would not be the right way for them to deal with this problem. That would be very cruel."

In this conversation, you have reassured your friend of your interest in him and his problem. But, at the same time, you have planted in his mind some questions that he should — and probably will — wrestle with.

For an appraisal to be helpful, it should, as a rule, be dispassionate and nonjudgmental. Usually, such evaluations will be most helpful when shared with a close friend. However, you cannot afford to turn your back on others who come to you with their problems — it's shocking how many people in this world don't feel that they have *anybody* in whom to confide. Rely on *their* judgment of your capacity to counsel with them rather than your own.

Still, you have to be careful that you don't give pat answers based on a superficial understanding of the problem and the underlying causes. Also, you must resist the temptation to assume the role of a power figure, taking advantage of their moment of weakness. There is also a possibility that if you lead them into revealing too much of themselves, they may suffer embarrassment and thereafter avoid you.

Bear in mind, also, that you can suggest the person consult with someone else. This may be a mutual friend, or it may be professional help. When you enter the water to help a person in distress, some element of risk is inherent. Do not, however, become so caught up in the hero image that you plunge in over your head and try techniques for which you are not qualified, thereby placing the other person in even greater jeopardy.

Here's where "read" differs from "interpret." Sure, you can tell that Pete Green is depressed. That's to *read*. But what, if anything, can you do about it? That's to *interpret*.

To interpret is, as I suggested earlier, to pause in your climb. Take a breather and take stock. Look down

Step Six: Interpret

upon the slope below you and recall the experiences that have brought you to this point. Inventory your inner strength and outer resources. Study the incline above you with an eye to planning your assault. If there is doubt, debate the pros and cons of going on.

In your person-to-person communication experiences, interpretation permits you to review your circumstances and evaluate the future. It permits you to inquire, "Do I wish to continue in the direction I'm headed?"

If your answer is "yes," you do want to drive on, then you can employ interpretation as a tool to help you get to your destination. Through interpretation, you can learn whether you're tuned in or tuned out. You can evaluate whether you're succeeding or failing.

If you sense that things may not be going well, you can ask of yourself:

- Was my preparation adequate? Can I yet gather facts and gain insights into the problem? Can I find interesting, graphic ways to augment my declaration?
- Did I fail to listen? Am I listening now?
- Did I read the group (or individual) correctly before declaring, and am I missing something now?
- Do I have their (his) attention; if not, can I capture or recapture it?
- Did I come on too strong in my declaration, or was I too weak? Was I defensive? Can I let my fire show?
- How can I bring my efforts to fruition? Or, if success is not forthcoming, how can I appropriate for myself, and help others to appropriate, the benefits of this experience?

A self-confident stance breeds confidence in a group; a stance of "I'm OK, you're OK" strengthens the foundations of friendship. Your attitude toward yourself and others is vitally important.

In *Psycho-Cybernetics*, Maxwell Maltz says that the subconscious cannot differentiate between real success and imagined success. He says that every success, whether real or imagined, reinforces your self-image. So, cultivate the resources of imagining success, anticipating success, and acting out success within your mind. Keep on telling yourself, "I will succeed!" Or, to avoid the connotation of materialism, say, "I will make my contribution!"

However, I am not suggesting that you should hurl yourself against all blocks, bars, and barriers indiscriminately. When you confront one of the Busy B's, you have to decide whether you will try to surmount it, go around it, come back another day, or withdraw to pursue other goals. You make your decision on the basis of the relative importance of your goal and your interpretation of your circumstances.

"Interpret" is perhaps the most treacherous surface we will have crossed in taking our seven steps, but you cannot reach the mountaintop without traversing it.

One of the major pitfalls of interpretation is our inclination to view life purely as a "game won, lost, or tied" proposition. We all know that this perspective traps us. There's infinitely more to life than the score. Still, we want and need mileposts to tell us "how we're doing." How we interpret the mileposts and how we react to them is of infinite importance.

If you sense success, don't let it go to your head;

Step Six: Interpret

don't make a fool of yourself. Particularly, don't abuse your sense of power and run roughshod over a dissenting minority.

Although you will want to remain sensitive to other persons and their responses to you, do not let someone's evaluation of your performance (which may be a snap evaluation, at that) become imprinted in your self-conscious as gospel truth without first running the whole situation back through your computer. Test all the elements before you accept such a judgment.

If you interpret the episode fully and well and come to the conclusion that you have failed, do not confuse your defeat over a *project* or *issue* as the defeat of *yourself as a person*. Do not lash yourself; do not lash out at others.

There are occasions when the only wise and generous thing to do is to say, "This isn't working. Let's drop it and try something else. We've learned some things that we can use in later ventures, of which there will be plenty."

If you will deal fairly with *yourself*, it'll be easier for you to deal fairly with *others*. And if you deal responsibly and maturely with others, there's a much better chance of your being treated this way in return.

Interpretation is "getting it all together." Interpretation is "telling it like it is." Interpretation is answering the questions, "Who am I?" and "How am I doing?" That's *real* communication.

For Your Practice

1. In Step One, we talked about purpose, objectives, and goals. Your purpose is your sense of who you are and want to become; it is your life-stance. And, you will recall, your objectives and goals are expressions of your purpose — they spell out what you intend to *do* as a result of who you *are*. Objectives are broader than goals are, and usually objectives project further into the future.

With this background, restate *your* purpose. Now list several of your objectives and/or goals. Having done this, take each objective/goal and interpret it. Is it in keeping with your purpose? Is it still viable? Have you made progress? What inner or outer forces stand in your way?

2. During the next twenty-four hours, practice *affirming*. Let the other person know that you recognize him as a person of value and that you are interested in and attentive to his achievements, aspirations, and disappointments. Find ways to establish closer identification through mention of experiences you hold in common.

3. Upon completing 2, above, repeat that exercise but add a heavy input of *reflective expressions*. Afterward, test the results:

   (a) Did you succeed in evidencing your interest and attention?
   (b) Did you draw the person out?
   (c) Did you find that use of reflective questions afforded you time for really hearing the other

Step Six: Interpret

person and for considering your own responses?

4. Select a person you've known well over a period of time — a family member, close friend, fellow worker. Picture him as he was one year, five years, or ten years ago, and then picture him now. In what respects has he changed? How did he get to be this way? Did his facility for, or lack of facility for, communication have anything to do with the changes? What do you see this person becoming in the future — say, ten years from now? Will communication likely have a significant influence upon his future?

5. In 4, above, how have the patterns of communication between yourself and this person changed? What changes do you expect in the future?

6. In connection with some group with which you are affiliated (business, religious, social, whatever), identify a project about which you have reservations. Do you think that it should have been undertaken? Do you think that it should be terminated — or continued? What forces do you see operating against its success? Is failure of communication one of the obstacles? How could communication be improved?

7. During your next experience with an organized group, evaluate how well the leader interprets. Does he periodically test the group to see if it understands what's going on and to see if the group is with him? What devices does he use in the way of interpretation? How could he improve his interpretative techniques?

8. During your next conversation of any considerable length, identify remarks made by the other person which are either critical of you personally or critical of

some idea, statement, or action of yours. Try to separate into two piles the remarks that are constructive, on the one hand, or that are too negative or superficial to be constructive, on the other. Watch yourself and see how well you interpret and respond.

9. Among your acquaintances with whom you have ongoing relationships, there is, no doubt, someone who continually (a) reiterates a prejudicial view, or (b) expresses hurt over an imagined insult or slight, or (c) expresses an inflated opinion either of himself generally or of some ability in particular. Give serious study to understanding the intent of the expression and the reasons for its repeated assertion. Would it be more helpful to the other person for you to continue to respond to the expression as you are doing, or to take a different tack? Try to take a more constructive approach in the future — but first, be sure you understand the potential consequences of such a move.

10. Continually test the "feedback" process to be sure your interpretation is being understood and accepted.

STEP 7
ASK FOR ACTION

In the person-to-person process there comes a time for action. When and how you call for action are crucial factors in whether or not your aspirations will be translated into reality. To ask for action is to say
- "Ready for the question?"
- "Will you participate in this project?"
- "Put your shoulder to the wheel."
- "Let's get on with it."

In a typical communication effort, you will have moved through the stages of preparation, listening, gaining attention, "reading," declaring, and interpreting. Very likely, the object of all this research, planning, mental juggling, and bargaining was to get someone to say either "no" or "yes." Chances are, you're counting on the one rather than the other. Should you ask for action *now*? What *form* should your call for action take?

To ask for action is to risk. They may say "no." And even if they say "yes," you may find yourself burdened with a large share of the responsibility for implementing the idea or program.

When and how you ask for action are bound up in
. Your goal
. Your priorities
. .Your resources
. The "temper" of the other person(s)
. External deadlines and other regulations

In Step One, we talked about the designing of *goals*. A goal is an expressed intention to achieve a well-defined result within a stated period of time. An example of a well-stated goal: "By putting John's overtime pay in a special savings account, we will finance a trip to Europe next spring." The *when* element is essential; it keeps a goal from being a mere *maybe-if* dream.

In the designing of proposed goals, which is a function of *preparation*, time is an important element. Time is also an important consideration in explaining and promoting proposed goals, which is *declaration*. Now we come to the final step, *asking for action*. Again, *timing* is essential. A goal which wins approval today might have been rejected if it had been brought to action yesterday. A goal which would be rejected today might win approval tomorrow.

Ideally, a goal will be compatible with the purpose and objectives of the organization or informal relationship. This compatibility should be designed into the goal. But while a group's purpose should have a dimension of durability in it, and its objectives should not undergo frequent flip-flops, there will be shifts in the interpretations of purpose and objectives. For example, a church group may be mission-minded today, whereas it was oriented toward Bible study six months ago. Another example: There was a time when banks clung to a conservative image and eschewed advertising (few went beyond the publication of a financial statement or a "card" stating they were still in business), but nowadays the advertising of some banks is as flamboyant as that of a hamburger chain.

In deciding when the call for action should be issued, one must give ample attention to priorities. Priorities are expressions of the relative values the group (or the other person) has assigned, either formally or informally, to needs, interests, and use of resources. (In looking at needs, I should mention that a *sense of oughtness* may affect the priority that is assigned a given project.)

If prevailing priorities were kept in mind back there in the design stage, they should not present difficulties in the *ask for action* stage. Actually, we tend to neglect our homework in the design stage — there isn't a sense of urgency until the time for commitment arrives. Besides, priorities are dynamic — they change.

There are psychological considerations as well as procedural considerations to be considered in deciding when to ask for action. What is the mood of the other person, or the group?

If you sense a wave of enthusiasm, you may want to guard against letting it wane. (You may also want to guard against giving the opposition time to rally its forces.) You may, therefore, choose to issue your call for action hard on the heels of your declaration.

If, on the other hand, you sense ambivalence, hostility, or confusion as to the facts and the issue, you may wish to delay action. (Your motivation may be your sense of responsibility, political considerations, or a mix of these and other influences.)

While you can usually anticipate the "climate" of a meeting, the "weather" is more problematic. For example, you may know that your group has been getting along wonderfully well with each other lately (that's climate) — but you may have no way of knowing that, during the week, two of your erstwhile lieutenants fell out with each other over a business deal (that's weather). Or, if you arrive for an appointment with Ms. Thomas, intending to persuade her to head a fund-raising campaign, and you find her tossing down two aspirin, you had better wait for a sunnier day.

In addition to those priorities which are intramural and which frequently afford a high degree of flexibility, there are external forces — deadlines and regulations among them — which narrow the options. These, too, influence strategy. If it will take your prospective date a month to obtain a gown, and the big dance is only five weeks away, then the time for you to act is now.

Timing is important. It's important in arts and crafts, sports and business activities. Timing is important in social interchange — dancing and romancing; it's important in religious activities — praying and preaching. In communication, timing can ensure or ruin your chances for success. The process *must* move along in a logical and harmonious fashion — each communication venture will

Step Seven: Ask For Action

have its own, peculiar rhythm. And, when the "moment of truth" arrives, the call for action must be sounded deliberately and gracefully, and it must fit into the framework of the earlier activities.

Will you marry my *idea*? Will you marry my *organization*? Will you marry *me*? These are important questions, and they deserve proper timing. The call for action should come at precisely the right moment — not too soon, not too late.

Sometimes, when there has already been too much dilly-dallying, a forthright approach must be taken.

There was this lady who saw herself entering old-maidhood. She had been dating this fellow for more than a decade, but she despaired of his dropping (much less *popping*) the question. So she decided to take the matter into her own hands. The next night, she confronted her low-key suitor with this high-key call for action:

"Do you think," she said, "that we ought to get married on the *first* Sunday in June or the *second* Sunday?"

Taking a cue from O. Henry, I'm not going to tell you whether or not the lady's call for action brought the desired result. (I might get the blame if readers tried the tactic and it failed them.)

There will be other occasions when the declaring will take a long span of time and the call for action must be held in abeyance. Let me describe such a situation:

A banker in a small North Carolina community conceived a dream for a public golf course. At the outset, a golf course seemed as foreign to that rural area as an opera house. But the banker had come to love and appreciate golf as a great game and wholesome exercise, and he wanted his people to have the privilege of enjoying it. He also felt it would be a tourist attraction.

Most of the power structure in his county, and certainly the bulk of the population, didn't know a putter from a niblick (indeed, they didn't know there was such a thing as a "niblick"). So, the banker couldn't appear summarily before the county commission and ask them, cold, to build a golf course. Nor could he expect to finance a course through subscriptions.

The banker contented himself with the role of a change agent. Slowly, he educated the people. Every chance he got, he took an influential person to a golf course — ideally, to play. Those who became acquainted with the game became enthusiastic over its pleasures and healthful effects. Also, bit by bit, he overcame the prejudices which are inherent in a country fellow's view of city slicker pastimes.

With prolonged nudging, public opinion shifted from good-natured jibes of "Do you know what that crazy banker wants to build here — a *golf course*!" to proud declarations of "We're going to have a golf course!" When the banker had brought public opinion to this point, he had to rely upon the people's confidence in his business integrity and judgment to obtain the execution of his plan.

Not so long ago, the banker took me to view the golf course. Here were mountain people — men, women, and youngsters — enjoying the game of golf. Among them were visitors, some of whom had driven many miles for the opportunity of playing on such an attractive course in such a breathtaking setting. And despite the rea-

Step Seven: Ask For Action

sonableness of the grounds fee, the course was paying its own way.

How much time had the banker allowed for *declaring* and, finally, *calling for action? Nine years!*

"And it was worth every minute of it," he commented.

In history, there are many instances where a person waited a lifetime to obtain action on his dream. There are numerous, though fewer, episodes where hundreds and even thousands of years elapsed between the dream and the reality. I'll acknowledge that most of us aren't keen about those kinds of waits, but perhaps their example will encourage us to be patient for a few hours or for a few days.

We've been talking about *when* to call for action. Now let's turn to *how*.

Rarely, an occasion may arise where the surprise element and the directness of blurting out your call for action will have a certain appeal. Usually, however, you will fare better if you have "set the stage."

One effective stage-setting method is to engage in *grooming talk*. Grooming talk comes in two major varieties, the *idea-building* type and the *ego-building* type.

In idea-building grooming talk, you may review the essentials of your declaration and give your interpretation of the current situation. You may picture the benefits which would ensue with the approval of the proposal.

Ego-building grooming talk appeals to the self-image of the decision-making group: "I've never known this group to let the children of this community down." Or, "This project is vital to the welfare of our citizens, and you are just the group to undertake it." You remind the group that they are experienced, wise, affluent, respected — or whatever other admirable characteristic may be pertinent and deserved. In Dr. Thomas Harris' book *I'm OK, You're OK*, the term for grooming talk is "stroking." It speaks of OK-ness. What you're saying is, "I'm OK, and you're OK. My proposition is OK, too. Further, it'll be OK for you to adopt it. Beyond this, your approval will enhance your OK-ness."

How effective an appeal for action will be may depend upon a great many factors — among them, for example, the historical context of the issue and the tone in which the request is made.

An employer walks into his secretary's office at 4:30 on a Friday and says, "Miss Johnson, I need to dictate two letters and they should go out this afternoon . . ."

The historical context will affect Miss Johnson's response. If this is the employer's habit, then Miss Johnson's connecting the current request with past episodes may make of it "the straw that broke the camel's back." But if Miss Johnson is the philosophical type, she may have learned to accept these situations with a shrug of "That's just the way he is so I might as well accept it." Or, if she is an independent type, she may lecture him and win a reprieve — or at least vent her feelings.

How the employer phrases his request will also influence the response. He might explain why it's so important for these particular letters to go out immediately.

If he is a sensitive type, he will inquire of the secretary

Step Seven: Ask For Action

what her personal situation is. In this event (let's assume), he would learn that Miss Johnson was about to ask him to let her off fifteen minutes early in order for her to prepare for a dinner date and an evening at the opera. We are getting into all kinds of impulses and reactions. In addition to an initial declaration, interpretation, and call for action, we have *counter* declarations, interpretations, and calls for action — perhaps the boyfriend gets into the act.

Calls for action and the responses may reflect the complicatedness of the relationship.

"When you finish your dessert, please take out the garbage." Will this request by a wife draw compliance or resistance. If compliance, will it be cheerful or grudging? We don't know enough about the two people or their moods to answer. Is the husband sensitive about his wife's "directing" him? Is taking out the garbage a recurrent source of antagonism? In the context of the particular evening, is the request "loaded," whereas on another night it might be free of emotional implications?

Would you have advised the wife to wait until after dessert to ask for action? If the garbage-toting is ordinarily the wife's chore, should she have offered to "trade off" with the husband by doing "his" chore? Should she identify her request as "special"? Might she couple the request with mention of a treat she has planned?

If you were the husband, would you have "read" your wife's day; would you, by dessert time, have brought your own cares of the day under control? If you had a deep-seated aversion to the garbage task, perhaps because it fell your lot as a kid, would you acknowledge this hang-up and offer to trade off with the wife, doing another chore instead?

When and *how* — and *if*. These can be complex questions.

For a request for action to have impact, it must hold significance.

- A request for students to do their homework must hold a promise of knowledge.
- An admonition expressed in a sermon must promise a more rewarding life.
- A television commercial must show wherein the advertised product or service will fill a need.

People are bombarded with thousands of appeals for their dollar, their endorsement, their participation. Persuasive messages are encountered on every hand. "Take action — buy — join — reform — share — impress — win!"

With so many appeals in the air, the competition is terrific. How can you stir someone into action?

For maximum appeal, your call for action must:

- *Imply confidence that the request will be granted and that the goal will be reached.* A wavering or perfunctory request encourages a response of, "If it doesn't make any more difference than that to him, why should I be concerned?"
- *Point to satisfactory performance in the past.* It's hard to overcome the stigma of failure. There will be a credibility gap if, on a previous occasion, you cried "Wolf!" when, actually, it was just a rabbit.
- *Have the right emotional tone.* The subject and the circumstances will dictate whether your pitch should be high-key or low-key, reassuring, or disturbing, straight or humorous. A tearful plea isn't appropriate for selling printing supplies, but it may

be just the thing for obtaining support for a children's hospital.
- *Be clearly stated and to the point.* Remember, you aren't declaring (you've already done that), you are clinching. So make every minute and every word count. Hone the cutting edge of your appeal. Beware of ambiguity. Do not hesitate to come right out and ask the person to sign on the line, share his testimony, give his money. Do not be coy or evasive. If your declaration was right on, the other person will be expecting a call for action.
- *Convey a spirit of mutual respect.* No "Big I, little u." Rather, your pitch must have an ego-building, relationship-cementing appeal.
- *Promise benefits — ideally, mutual benefits.* Ordinarily, you wouldn't stress how much the action will help *you*, but how it will help *me*, or help us in association with others.
- *Be expressed in terms of people.* An advertisement for a typewriter may stress technical superiority — clarity of type, speed of performance, low cost of maintenance. Still, the manufacturer recognizes that the typist may participate in the decision-making, so he will include a "human" pitch as well.
- *Be free of false urgency.* Don't use a hard-sell approach when a soft-sell approach will do. Bring the group to make its *own* decision rather than buying *your* package. Duress leaves a bitter taste. If a community's water source is contaminated, it's proper to sound an alarm — but a golf course? (Recall the patient groundwork which led to that course in rural North Carolina!)

You have led the other person down the communication road, to the fork. It's time to ask him to make a decision. It may or may not be your role to tell him *which* route to take, but if the choice is clear to you and you feel obligated to give direction, do so with confidence.

Columbus went to the Queen and asked for money to make a trip. Legend has it she was so impressed that she sold her jewels to finance the voyage. History was changed. What if Columbus had not had the courage to face the Queen and ask for support?

The great leaders of the Judeo-Christian tradition frequently went to the people and demanded that they make choices. Remember the story of Joshua. The 24th chapter of the book of Joshua relates that in a time of crisis, Joshua exhorted: "Choose this day whom you will serve."

The greatest movement that the world has seen, the establishment and growth of the Christian Church, was based on a few simple requests for action: "Follow me and I will make you become fishers of men" (Mark 1:17 RSV) said Jesus to Simon, later to be named Peter the Rock.

At various times, Jesus laid down challenges in these words: "Come" — "follow" — "go" — "tell."

The Good Lord expects us to ask, and to ask with *confidence* and *expectation*. This is the secret of good communication. The greatest motivating statement of all is this simple statement of promise:

"Ask, and it will be given you; seek, and you will find; knock, and it will be opened to you." (Matthew 7:7 RSV)

Great expectation — positive affirmation — simple language. And done on a person-to-person basis. That's communication at its best!

For Your Practice

1. During the last twenty-four hours, did you forfeit a good opportunity to "ask for action"? Why did you? Was it a lack of time — a lack of nerve? Did you cop out because to ask the other person for action would have placed a burden on him — or on you? Is the appeal still worth making? If so, lay plans now to make it tomorrow or in the near future.

2. Each of us has had experience with fund-raising enterprises, either as a solicitor or as a prospect. Reflect upon a specific campaign — maybe the latest every-member canvass of your church or the latest solicitation for your community's one-pledge fund. Evaluate the way that the solicitor (*you*, if applicable) asked for action. Were the timing and content of the appeal good or bad? Why do you judge it so?

3. While watching television, keep a pad handy and jot down the key words that are employed in calls for action. (Don't get hung up on *declarations*, which are something else.) Concerning each of these requests for action, make these judgments:

    (a) Was the appeal clear, direct, and to the point?
    (b) Was it made with vigor and enthusiasm?
    (c) Was the pitch emotional or intellectual? Was it appropriate?
    (d) Was there a heavy "you" appeal? Did it suggest that you are important? Did it promise benefits for you? Mutual benefits?
    (e) What improvements would you suggest?

Step Seven: Ask For Action   121

4. While listening to a sermon, church school lesson, or other talk, mentally underline requests for action. Read through some editorials in newspapers or magazines and underscore requests for action. In both categories, were you surprised to find many (or few) appeals? Do you think that the modern preacher, lecturer, and/or editorialist makes *harder* (or *softer*) pitches for action than did their predecessors? Is this shift desirable?

5. Mothers and wives are sometimes characterized as being inclined to nag. (I gladly testify that it isn't just the womenfolk who nag!) Does nagging reflect an inability to make a definite and direct request for action?

6. Do you recall an instance in which you called for action prematurely? What were the consequences? Do you recall an instance where you should have called for action earlier than you did? What were the consequences?

7. In the next group activity in which you are engaged, watch for calls for action and conjecture whether the calls might have been more effective at an earlier or later time.

8. In your day-to-day activities, listen for your requests for action from the people with whom you are associated. Consider whether or not you might improve these requests in terms of timing and content.

9. In instances such as those you encountered in 8, above, try ego-building grooming talk. Is it difficult to arrive at the proper balance between compliments that are appropriate and deserved, on the one hand, and those which are too syrupy and exaggerated, on the other?

ADDENDUM I

I hope you have appropriated my methodology for person-to-person communication and have already used it in many areas of your life. I'm confident that if you have done the exercises at the end of each chapter, you have mastered each step.

My deeper hope, however, is that your investment of time and effort is paying off in terms of enriched relationships and personal fulfillment. And, beyond this, that the seven steps have been so enjoyable and so productive that you are waiting eagerly to take the thousands of steps available to you in the future. I promised that these seven steps would bring you to a more effective level of person-to-person communication, and I hope you have attained it. However, the journey has just begun.

All along, I asked you to *reach out*. Not to reach out merely for the purpose of selling someone a bill of goods, but for the purpose of gaining something for yourself and others. Listening, "reading," and interpreting suggest reflection, introspection, digestion, assimilation.

Addendum I

The rewards that flow from quiet, unhurried, and even solitary activity are so great that I feel I should emphasize them again just now. I think you will acknowledge that we are individually egocentric and that our society is action-oriented and achievement-oriented, and these qualities can lead us into trouble. When you consider the term "person-to-person communication," I think it only natural for you to assume that the first "person" refers to you and the second "person" to somebody else. This is okay, of itself, but you are about to cheat yourself if you make another assumption: that the action (the communication) must flow from the first person to the second person. True, the order of the sentence suggests it, but don't you believe it! The flow is in both directions!

Another thing I'd like to stress is that the person-to-person process is also a *personal* process.

I've encouraged you to visit with the other person in his castle, but you and he must — and will — remain *two* persons. You can mix and mingle, but eventually you must return to your own castle.

You must learn to live with other people — and communication is the key. But you must also learn to live with yourself — and, again, communication is the key. You must take time out from the busyness of your life to communicate with yourself.

Although self-actualization is still another book, I'd like to interpret here, very briefly, the person-to-person process in "first person" terms.

I have to prepare. I have to be still and hear what it is that God proposes for me to say, do, and *be*. Not to project any agenda for my whole lifetime, necessarily, but for this hour, this day. I must develop a life-position, objectives, and goals. What do I want to give and receive? What do I want to *become*? Do I want to be a financial success, a wiser man, a better Christian? I must have *direction*. I must plan.

Do I value myself highly enough to take the time to "listen" to *me* and to "read" *myself*? (Maybe I don't even gain my own attention.) Do I know my moods? Have I learned how to break out of depression, which may stem from monotony, or from a slight or an insult? (The secret is to fix my interest on something — someone — outside myself.)

In the field of declaring, have I delineated the principles by which I propose to live, or do I prefer to live in the shadowy, gray area? Am I able to stand tall and say, "This I believe, and this I will pursue"?

Do I interpret myself and my situations fairly, or am I inclined to brand into my forehead the words "Mistake Maker"? Am I willing to probe objectively into the causes for my guilt feelings and my sense of failure? Do I try to understand what it is that I am running away from?

Do I back away from calling other people to action because I can't bring myself to act? Do I procrastinate and vacillate, retreating from the moment of decision to engage in repetitious and superfluous declaring and interpreting?

To be successful in *person-to-person* communication, you have to understand that *first* person — who he is, what he has to give, what he needs.

Addendum I

Think of what you are today and how you got to be this way. No doubt, communication has had a lot to do with it. Now, think of what you want to become. Communication can contribute immensely to the achievement of your objectives.

Don't expect wonders in a week or a month. You can't change radically in short order — and radical change isn't what you're after, very probably. If you're a mousy type, you may never become a back-slapping type — you wouldn't feel comfortable at it. But communication can help you to acquire whatever dimension it is you seek. You tend to become what you think about, talk about, hear about. You tend to be like the persons with whom you communicate.

As the janitor of our opening chapter said, "You got to want to." And I hope the seven steps that we have taken together have imbued you with sufficient want-to for you to aspire to continue your journey toward more effective — more fulfilling — communication. The journey will take time and effort, sure, but think of the rewards: enrichment of your own mind and soul — the enrichment of others' lives!

E. J. McClanahan, who was at the time president of the Western Operations Division of the Standard Oil Company, said that for optimum development of human relations and interpersonal communication, there are three requisites:

. The ability to prepare
. The ability to present
. The ability to persevere

Persevere! Learn all you can of the principles of person-to-person communication. Learn all you can about people. Study individuals. Be inventive and develop your own methods. Practice. But remember: It's *what* you communicate that counts most. Ask yourself, "What do the people around me — in my home, neighborhood, place of work, the broader community — what do they need most?" You can ascertain their real needs, and fill many of these needs, if you will relate to them as persons of value rather than as persons in roles.

There's the other person, in his castle, looking out toward you and your castle. You can greet him warmly, or reject him. You can invite him in, or shut him out.

There the other person is, and here you are. Between the two of you are those moats. But there are also drawbridges. The drawbridges represent opportunities for communication, for sharing, for growth.

It doesn't take much effort to go and let down the drawbridge of communication. Just seven steps. Seven steps, and a wonderful journey begins!

And the reward lies not alone in achieving the destination; the strength of the reward lies within the joy of the journey!

Together, we've taken our seven steps:

Ask for Action
Interpret
Declare
Gain Attention
"Read"

Listen

Prepare

ADDENDUM II

Ten Commandments of Christian Communication

I

Thou shalt remember the gifts the Lord thy God hath given thee, which are multiplied and made useful in our lives as the Holy Spirit communicates to us the power and will of God.

II

Thou shalt recognize that the Lord thy God shares his gifts with us as we learn to accept and communicate with persons — persons whom God has endowed with intelligence and the capacity and ability to become.

III

Thou shalt cultivate the gifts of seeing, hearing, touching, smelling, and tasting as the sensory gifts by which we receive and process information from the world in which we live.

IV

Thou shalt value the priceless and unique gift of the voice with which we communicate our words, ideas, and emotions.

V

Thou shalt learn to respect the person who speaks to you, learning to see, to hear, and to understand the message he seeks to share with you.

VI

Thou shalt understand that Christian communication leads to Christian experiences, and these endow our imagination and our memory with moments of truth, beauty, and goodness, which become priceless treasures for now and eternity.

VII

Thou shalt remember the purpose of communication is to increase understanding, and as we seek to understand, so shall we be understood.

VIII

Thou shalt be aware that no communication takes place until each person knows and uses words, symbols, and codes that are a part of the common knowledge of those who participate in a two-way traffic of communication.

IX

Thou shalt cherish the tongue and the voice as instruments of integrity, and never debase these gifts by using them for lying, gossiping and/or bearing false witness; for the sin of communication is to use persons and the communication process for a selfish end.

X

Thou shalt love, honor, and obey the Lord thy God, who, in his love, communicates himself by the gift of the Divine Symbol — the Word made Flesh — so that man can know what God is like and know that he still communicates his love to us as we listen and obey; for through prayer we seek communion with him, and prayer is the communicative art of listening, understanding, and obeying the Voice of God.

J. W. S.